WALKING INTO THE LYONS' DEN

I was in a bit of a quandary, for I felt I ought to sound older than my employers, and up till then I had mostly played very young parts. I always seem to find two ways of doing parts, each quite different from the other. So it was with Aggie. I suggested to Bebe that if I played her with a low, warm voice I would sound couthy, sympathetic, and old. So I did the first reading this way.

Bebe shook her head. 'No, that's not right, honey.' Ben looked distinctly worried.

But I had the other voice up my sleeve. Or rather in my memory. The high shrill voice of the old lady who had so amused us on our holiday in Jersey in October, and which Sandy had advised me to keep tucked away for future use, because I could imitate it so well. Now was the moment. 'Och well, Mrs Lyon, maybe you'd rather I did it like this,' and I screeched in a high falsetto, ending up with a laugh like a skirl of the bagpipes.

'That's it. That's the one,' declared a delighted Bebe and Ben, and that was the start of a voice and of an association which was to last for a decade.

Molly Weir

WALKING INTO
THE LYONS' DEN

ARROW BOOKS

Arrow Books Limited
3 Fitzroy Square, London W1P 6JD

An imprint of the Hutchinson Publishing Group

London Melbourne Sydney Auckland
Wellington Johannesburg and agencies
throughout the world

First published Hutchinson 1977
Arrow edition 1979
© Molly Weir 1977

Made and printed in Great Britain
by The Anchor Press Ltd
Tiptree, Essex

ISBN 0 09 919440 6

FOR BEBE

Her Yea was Yea, and her Nay Nay.
And we were safe in the certainties
Of her whole character.

ISABEL FRY

Do every job as if it were the only one you'll be
judged by.

SIR WALTER SCOTT

There's nothing worth the wear of winning,
but laughter and the love of friends.

HILAIRE BELLOC

1

It was the night before Hogmanay, 1949.

I put the milk bottle out and looked up at the stars.

Sandy and I had been living in our comfortable little house on the outskirts of London for nearly six months, and had revelled in the heat of a real English summer, but it still felt strange to be so far away from 'home'. We both knew in our bones that wherever we chose to hang up our hats, Scotland would always be home to us.

At first I had really felt like Ruth among the alien corn, and somehow this sense of alienation was always strongest when I heard the chink of the milk bottle on an English doorstep. Surrounded as we were by English voices, by neighbours who were charming and welcoming but who showed a total lack of curiosity about one another, a characteristic which seemed quite foreign to us, I couldn't get used to the fact that nobody in the whole street really knew me, and that I could walk the mile to the station without a friendly voice to call out hullo.

I was later to value this live-and-let-live attitude, this respect for the privacy of others, especially when I started writing in earnest and solitude was essential, but just then it seemed a disorientating thing to be cut off from my homeland and without any strong ties to bind me to my new country.

Later I was also to look back with amazement tinged

with slight regret for this peaceful anonymity, when I became such a well-known face that I couldn't enter a bus or a shop without the entire place coming to a standstill.

But all that lay ahead in the mists which shrouded the New Year.

I felt very conscious that Sandy and I had replaced one very old lady who had formerly lived in our house in that quiet lane, and all summer I had tried not to laugh or talk too enthusiastically in the garden for fear of disturbing the tranquillity of the somewhat elderly neighbours.

But Hogmanay is a great Scottish occasion, and I'd decided to risk being accused of unseemly and riotous behaviour and had asked the immediate neighbours to come in at midnight, to bring in the New Year with us. We were the only Scots in the lane, and the first Scots ever to have suggested such a thing to them, and they thought it a great lark. At that time it was only in Scotland that New Year's Day was a public holiday, by tradition, and the holiday was essential not only to recover from the all-night revelry, but for everyone to pay calls on friends and relatives who hadn't been out first-footing to wish them the compliments of the season over a festive drink.

We were aware the Sassenachs hadn't yet cottoned on to this civilized custom, and that we would have to face the unpleasant prospect of work next day, a prospect which slightly took the edge off the uninhibited nature of the revels, which would certainly have to be curtailed to allow us to get some sleep.

Sandy, never fond of parties at any time, was aghast at my temerity in filling the house with English neighbours who knew nothing of Hogmanay or its customs. He was gloomily certain they'd dislike the whole thing. He was also very anxious that, not knowing the drill, the visitors would also be ignorant of the acceptability of leaving after half an hour, once the New Year toasts had been drunk and we'd honoured the departure of the old year. This was normal practice in Scotland, of course, where first-foots went from house to house, each visit lasting only a short time, and where the success of the occasion was measured by the number of houses visited, and the number of friends and bottles accounted for between the stroke of midnight and, if stamina held out, breakfast-time on Ne'erday.

In Scotland nobody stayed for very long at any one house for this reason, and the streets were filled with revellers carrying bottles, wending their way to friends and calling out to everyone, 'A Happy New Year', which met with the response, 'The same tae yersel'.'

'What will we do if they don't go?' he persisted. 'After all, I've got to be up for work in the morning.'

'Well, so have they,' I pointed out. 'They'll want to get to bed too – don't be silly.'

Midnight came and with it the neighbours, giggling and pushing but duly armed with the slice of bread and piece of coal I'd warned them to bring, to ensure our new home would be blessed with food and warmth for the coming year.

They also remembered my other command, and pushed in the blackest-haired member of the party first, doubly ensuring our good luck for the year. I produced whisky and wine, cake and shortbread, and we toasted the New Year, and chatted . . . and chatted . . . and chatted.

My husband looked at me desperately. The visitors looked at me expectantly. I couldn't very well call, 'Time, ladies and gentlemen, please.' It was quite clear from their faces that they expected far more than this quiet celebration. Weren't the Scots famous for their wild orgies, north of the Border? I felt I was letting the side down terribly, with not so much as a haggis, or a squeak from a bagpipe.

9

'What about a tune on the piano?' I said weakly, avoiding Sandy's eye.

One of the visitors turned out to be a wizard player, and we all gathered round the piano and voices rang out merrily, while the hands of the clock crept round. I was sure there would be a banging on the door from irate neighbours further along the lane, with all this uninhibited community singing, but my hitherto quiet neighbours seemed delighted to be letting their hair down in true Scottish style!

Somebody murmured plaintively he felt hungry with all this unaccustomed revelry in the middle of the night. Ignoring Sandy's pleading looks, and his significant glance at the clock, I went into the kitchen and quickly made a pile of sandwiches from the remains of the turkey, loaded a plate with more cake and shortbread, and brewed two pots of tea. The food was greeted with rapturous cries from the party, and gave them a second wind for more singing, and even a spot of dancing.

An elderly mother, clutching a glass of port to her bosom, gazed at me with starry eyes and flushed cheeks, and said it was the liveliest night she'd had for years. I could well believe her, for the only other times I'd seen her in the street were when she was making her slow and careful way to the post office for her pension, and she always drew fearfully aside as though the mere breeze of one's passing would topple her.

It was five a.m. when we said our farewells, and nearer six by the time we'd tidied the room and washed the dishes and put everything away. We couldn't start the year by leaving a sink full of dirty dishes. That would have been the most terribly bad luck as well as being downright sluttish.

When we passed the neighbours next morning on our way to the station, they seemed quite proud of their Hogmanay hangovers, and were obviously all set to boast how they were kept out of bed by the mad Scots next door.

Sandy, half asleep, was already making plans for the next Hogmanay. 'Let's stick to people who know the ropes next time,' he groaned, 'or leave it till Hogmanay is on a Friday or a Saturday and we can have a long lie next day.'

But it was a marvellous way to get to know the neighbours, and following the old Scottish rituals certainly brought me the greatest piece of luck I could have dreamed of, right out of the blue.

The luck didn't come immediately, but then we Scots know the year lasts twelve months, and we're not averse to waiting, just so long as it comes! I didn't often go into town 'to do the rounds', visiting producers and directors, and hanging around the pubs where those arbiters of our fate were wont to be found. For one thing I still had the Scottish feeling of intense guilt at going into a public house. How often had I heard my mother saying, when I was a wee girl, 'Aye, she's the lowest of the low, she goes into pubs and stauns aboot wi' a' the men.' No respectable woman in Springburn would have crossed the threshold of a public house, and I couldn't shake off the feeling that drinking in such 'dens of iniquity', as Grannie called them, was the sure road to hell.

And yet in London nobody blinked an eye at the sight or sound of a female asking for a tomato juice or a gin and tonic, and it was the surest way of bumping into BBC types out for a noggin at lunchtime. So, very cautiously, I was occasionally persuaded by an actress friend to 'do the rounds' and try to drum up a little work for myself. As she truly said, 'If they never see you, they just forget you.' They'd now forgotten me for three months.

So, on this particular day, I had made a date to meet her at the bar round the corner from Aeolian Hall, the home of

BBC Light Entertainment, but to my dismay she didn't turn up. I stood it as long as I could, feeling (in the words of dear Tommy Handley) as out of place as a pork pie at a Jewish wedding, clumsily holding my tomato juice, smiling brightly all round to pretend I felt at home, and then, self-consciousness overcoming my pretended poise, I turned and fled.

I nearly knocked Tom Ronald over, and as he steadied me with a 'Whoa, watch where you're going', he recognized me as the Scot he'd used to replace a busier actress who couldn't manage the Scots accent for her part in the Cicely Courtneidge series *The House Next Door* earlier that year.

'What are you doing just now, Molly?' he asked.

I didn't let on that I'd been 'resting' for a good three months, but just assumed the carefree laughter of a busy actress without a care in the world. 'Oh, I'm free as a bird at the moment,' I said, craftily, leaving him to assume that he was lucky to catch me at an idle moment! I don't suppose he was taken in for a second. We all behaved like this.

'How would you like to do a trial recording with Bebe and Ben?' he said.

I gasped.

'You don't mean Bebe Daniels and Ben Lyon?' I said, hardly able to believe my ears, and very impressed by his use of their Christian names to me, as though I moved in their circles.

He nodded.

'When?' I said.

'Next Monday evening, at Piccadilly 1.'

'I'll be there,' I said.

'We'll ring you later and give you the exact time,' he said. 'I have your number, haven't I, because we rang you when you helped us out with Cis Courtneidge.' So he *had* remembered.

I wondered if he had intended to ask me for this trial recording or if it had just been bumping into me, or rather me bumping into him, which had triggered off the idea.

It was years before I found courage to test my theory that it had been the Hogmanay raven-haired first-foot who had brought me this chance. That talisman could possibly have set the wheels in motion, of course, but Tom's choice was based on far firmer foundations. It appeared that when discussions took place for actors for the trial recording Bebe insisted that the housekeeper must be Scottish. For three reasons. First, because employing a Scots cook was a real piece of oneupmanship for anyone who was anyone in Hollywood. Second, because with their shrewd awareness of all the angles of show business, Bebe and Ben wanted to encourage as wide a British public as possible, and they already had English members in mind for the other parts. And third, because Bebe's father was a Scot, a MacMeal from Edinburgh, and with her knowledge of Scotland and Scots ways she just refused to consider anyone 'putting on' a Scottish accent. It had to be the real Mackay.

Again, the Lyons preferred artists who had already proved themselves successful in other shows, and who were experienced in comedy. So when Tom suggested me (it wasn't long after *The House Next Door* recording that these discussions had taken place) and they had asked, 'Is she good? What has she done?' Tom was able to say, 'Well, she was with Tommy Handley in *ITMA*, and I used her recently in the Cis Courtneidge series.' They had only the vaguest recollection of having met me at the Grosvenor 'Tommy' awards, but the mere fact of having been in the *ITMA* series was enough.

Trial recordings were deadly serious affairs, for depending on their effect on the listening panel of top brass within the

BBC was the decision as to whether or not the show had possibilities as a series.

So casting was meticulous.

At that stage I didn't care a button whether it became a series or not. I was simply agog to meet the Lyons. The whole thing was done in complete secrecy, for no hint of a possible series was allowed to be leaked until the thing became a solid fact, so that there would be no bruised feelings. And so that the producer wouldn't be inundated with out-of-work actors battering his door down !

It was a cold, crisp evening when I went along to Piccadilly 1, and whatever the outcome I was starry-eyed to be introduced to the entire famous family: Bebe, beautiful with her enormous brandy-ball eyes, showgirl legs and exquisitely cut pale grey suit with snowy crêpe-de-chine blouse; Ben, tall, warm and handsome; Barbara, like a peach-fed Southern belle, with beautiful dark brown silky hair, narrower eyes than her mother's and of a lighter brown in shade, but with her father's hands, as I instantly noted, for on the engagement finger was the biggest diamond I'd ever seen in my life. Barbara, at nineteen, had just hit the headlines because she had become engaged to the son of the richest man in the world, George Getty, the son of Paul Getty of whom, till that moment, I'd never heard. Why should I, come to that? Millionaires then were quite outside my experience, unless they were Hollywood ones, or had some connection with show business. Oil millionaires occupied a fantasy world unknown to me.

She accepted everybody's congratulations with quiet 'Thank yous', which I thought very intriguing, being more used to the Scots responses of 'Aye, it's lovely, ma ring, isn't it?' instead of a deprecating 'You like it? Oh I'm so glad.' Who wouldn't like a magnificent diamond like that? I was fairly hypnotized and, still in a daze, turned to meet

14

Richard and saw a slim youngster of fifteen, very sharp, very American, and not like either of his parents. I wasn't aware he was an adopted son, but I was very aware, once we'd started rehearsing, of the strong feeling there was between him and Bebe. They continually threw one another laughing, loving glances, and it fairly warmed my heart to see them.

ITMA was well and truly represented in the cast for apart from myself there was my friend and dinner-companion, Hugh Morton ('Would you care for a sninch of puff?'), Horace Percival ('Dirty postcards, sir? Very spicy – oh crikey!'), and Doris Rogers, whose double booking had led to my being used in the Cicely Courtneidge show.

Bebe had very definite ideas of all our characters. Doris was to be Florrie, the next-door neighbour, who was at loggerheads with Ben and the butt of all his jokes against fat nosy women. Horace was Mr Wimple, the neighbour with the vast number of children. Hugh was to be the bank manager, Ben's boss, and any odd voices which were required. I was to be the housekeeper, Aggie, and Bebe emphasized I was to be a firm, determined, almost bossy character of whom the family were in considerable awe, with the sort of personality which indicated that if I wanted breakfast in bed, then they'd have to toe the line!

I was in a bit of a quandary, for I felt I ought to sound older than my employers, and up till then I had mostly played very young parts. I always seem to find two ways of doing parts, each quite different from the other. So it was with Aggie. I suggested to Bebe that if I played her with a low, warm voice I would sound couthy, sympathetic, and old. So I did the first reading this way.

Bebe shook her head. 'No, that's not right, honey.' Ben looked distinctly worried.

But I had the other voice up my sleeve. Or rather in my

memory. The high shrill voice of the old lady who had so amused us on our holiday in Jersey in October, and which Sandy had advised me to keep tucked away for future use, because I could imitate it so well.* Now was the moment. 'Och well, Mrs Lyon, maybe you'd rather I did it like this,' and I screeched in a high falsetto, ending up with a laugh like a skirl of the bagpipes.

'That's it. That's the one,' declared a delighted Bebe and Ben, and that was the start of a voice and of an association which was to last for a decade.

It took several weeks before the decision to do the series was taken, and I went through the usual traumas wondering first of all whether the BBC would accept *Life with the Lyons* as a series, and secondly, if they would accept *me* as the housekeeper, or if I would sound too young for the part. At last the telephone call came from Tom Ronald telling me I was indeed to be Aggie, and that rehearsals would start in early autumn. If I had been able to turn a somersault in our wee kitchen, I'd have done it, so ecstatic did I feel at having been booked for a trial six-week period with this legendary Hollywood couple and their family.

With the experience of *ITMA* behind me, I knew six-week contracts were quite usual, renewable at the end of each period, and that if the show turned out to be the success everybody predicted it would be, this was a mere formality. Of course the show itself might be top of the hit parade, but I could easily be found wanting, like poor Tony Francis in *ITMA*, who had only lasted for his trial six weeks. I determined not to worry about such dire possibilities, and to make the most of every single one of the first six shows, and to do my best to please producer and public so perfectly that the mere idea of doing without me would never enter their heads.

* *Stepping into the Spotlight*, Hutchinson, 1975.

Sandy was delighted too, for he knew that if the show lasted a year, there was no danger of my whizzing off to do another stage play, and he'd find a light in the window and a dinner on the table five nights out of seven!

I never realized how much he disliked returning to an empty house until one night a rehearsal was cancelled, and I opened the door to him, the smell of steak pie drifting past as I called out, 'Surprise, surprise, Richard was ill so we were all sent home.'

A smile transformed his face and he said, 'Oh, if I'd realized you were there, I wouldn't have dawdled up the road, I'd have hurried as fast as I could.'

My heart turned over. 'Do you mean to say,' I said wonderingly, 'that you take as long as possible to get to the house when you know I'm not going to be in?'

'Yes,' he said, affecting a careless air, and went upstairs to change while I finished off the last-minute preparations for our meal. I was quite staggered. He had always given me such warm and enthusiastic support for everything I did that it had never occurred to me he had to pay a price in loneliness which he kept at bay by sauntering home-wards when I was absent, and hurrying when I was there.

It was at that moment that I decided that if I were ever offered another stage play I would not accept it until I had a 'get-out' clause which would enable me to leave on giving two weeks' notice. And indeed I would never again actually look for theatre work, although I would have to consider it if a part were offered. I would concentrate on radio, TV and films, which would fit in much more acceptably to a united and happy married life.

I felt a bit better though when, over our steak pie, Sandy chuckled and said, 'Mind you, it's far better to get a rare surprise like this, than to get into a rut and take it for granted there'll always be a wife and a pie waiting every night when I get home.'

I laughed too. 'Aye, sailors' wives say it's one long honeymoon, only in this case *I'm* the sailor!'

We did the first six of the Lyons' shows from Aeolian Hall in Bond Street, and they were an immediate success. This was the first time a real family had appeared as themselves, supposedly in their own home, with the housekeeper, the neighbours, the bank manager and all the ramifications of family life which provided immediate identification with every family in the land. It was of course larger than life, but it *sounded* like any family, and soon people were making a point of listening to us every week, and sometimes listening to the repeat on Sundays as well, to make sure of missing nothing.

Bebe was thrilled to the core on being asked if we could possibly change the time of our Sunday repeat, so that the children could listen to us and then go on to Sunday school! This request came from the ministers of the many churches who were finding that children were skipping Sunday school because *Life with the Lyons* came on too late for them to hear us *and* get to Sunday school on time. Bebe felt this was truly the accolade that we were indeed what she had aimed for, 'a good clean family show'. And the repeat time was duly changed.

She was an absolute perfectionist. She devised the story lines, decided which scenes her two fellow writers would tackle, and which ones she would do herself. She disappeared into her office 'down the dunney' in the basement, **and** only surfaced when she was almost forcibly yanked upstairs to eat at the end of the normal person's working day. As soon as she had eaten, she headed for the basement again, to check and re-check what she had written, to discuss with her co-writers what *they* had written, and to read to the family the completed scenes for an immediate reaction.

On the occasions when I went to the house to read scripts, which we frequently did at the beginning of the series, the place fairly hummed with activity and it was like one huge, non-stop party. There would be the Lyons family of course, the two co-writers, Bob Block and Ronnie Hanbury, and later a third, Bill Harding. Bebe's mother, Bunny, would be popping out and in. All the regular members of the cast would be there, plus any odd voices, notably Gwen Lewis who came in from time to time as Mrs Wimple, and David Enders who played a variety of young men in the life of Barbara. Then there would be various members of the fan club, who listened to rehearsals and provided reactions, and at least two secretaries, a man who did various errands such as collecting groceries or cigarettes, or passing orders to the cook, and friends of Richard and Barbara who waited patiently until we'd finished before going out for the rest of the evening.

I'd never imagined such frenzied activity could go on in an ordinary house, or that life could be lived with so many people around all the time. But then, of course, this was no 'ordinary' house. This was Life with the Lyons, lived both in front of the public and behind the scenes. This was pure Hollywood, where the stars were constantly encircled by a whole constellation of stardust and where privacy was almost unknown. When I remembered with what passion I had schemed to have a room of my own, and had scrimped and saved to help my mother pay the extra rent demanded for this dreamed-of private place,* I was amazed that people in their position could deliberately choose to be surrounded by a small army of assistants from dawn till dusk, so that they were seldom if ever alone. Later, when I got to know more Americans, I came to the conclusion that this wasn't so much a Lyons characteristic as an American one, and it

* *Best Foot Forward*, Hutchinson, 1972.

was no surprise then to learn that Bob Hope had a platoon of writers from whom he was scarcely ever separated, that Sinatra had his little band of friends always on hand, and that every top film-maker had no less than half a dozen people in constant attendance. It was a revelation with the Lyons, though, just as was their capacity for sheer professionalism and hard work.

Although we all loved what we were doing, we British had a far more casual attitude to broadcasting. I had to admit it. If a rehearsal was called for three-thirty, the first thing any of us did was drift towards the tea-bar to collect a cup of something and a biscuit before so much as opening a script. This used to drive Ben mad, as well as mystify him that we could behave like this. He was used to American zest and competitive keenness, and it wasn't long before we learned that if everyone was to be kept happy and sweet-tempered then we'd better have our tea swallowed and that biscuit consumed, all ready to go straight into rehearsal at the appointed hour. He was absolutely right, of course. It was this businesslike approach which made shows from the USA so slick and accident-proof.

Other radio stars used to ask me, in awed tones, how many hours we rehearsed for our half-hour show, and were stunned to hear we did a whole evening's work, followed by steady rehearsing on the day of the recording, from mid-afternoon until eight o'clock. Members of the public, on the other hand, thought we just picked up the script and read it from sight!

The minute I had my script handed to me I flew through the pages, marking my part, and checking that my dialogue sounded Scottish. Anything in the least jarring halted me in my tracks. Bebe would be looking at me with a quizzical smile.

'Well?' she would ask.

'Bebe,' I would begin hesitantly, 'can I change something?'

'Why, honey?' she would ask, with a tiny wink to the others.

'Well, you see,' and I'd clear my throat nervously, 'we wouldn't say it like that in Scotland.'

The ensuing laughter would have me blushing to the roots of my hair.

'How do you like that little Aggie?' she would demand of the others. 'We only take the entire darn week to write the script and the moment she takes a look at it, all that hard work goes for nothing because "We wouldn't say it like that in Scotland".'

She was only teasing. If there was one quality Bebe appreciated above all others it was enthusiasm, and she knew that any suggestions from me came from my sole desire to have a perfect script. And, having had a Scottish father, the last thing in the world she wanted was phoney Scots. Eventually I appointed myself unofficial 'audience reaction' during rehearsals, and I'd lay down my script and simply listen. In this way I was able to distinguish the 'written' joke from the aural one, which isn't always an easy distinction to make when one has been too closely associated with the written script.

I'd go up to Bebe and whisper, 'That's not a radio joke, Bebe. It has to be *read* to get its meaning, and the audience aren't reading, they're listening, and they won't get it.' She was all attention. The other writers would be called over, a swift adjustment made, and the laugh more strongly ensured when our audience heard it later that evening. I was very nervous when I first made such suggestions but Bebe was enchanted to feel I was so interested, and brought a fresh ear to a script which for her had become all too familiar by this time. Mind you, the fact that I too wrote may have helped me not to get a dusty answer for being cheeky enough to stick my oar in!

Ben was absolutely marvellous at 'warming up' an audience, an essential part of the evening's success. Many people were in a studio for the first time, and felt strange and awkward and overawed. The 'warm-up' was to put them at their ease and have them laughing and relaxed by the time the red light warned us the clock was ticking round to recording time.

He gagged with them mercilessly. He made somebody wearing gloves stand up in front of the entire audience and apologize for clapping with her gloves on! He would remove a fur coat, most solicitously, from a lady, then rush to Bebe with it and drape it round her shoulders, saying, 'Here you are, honey, this will be perfect for you to wear going home!'

He introduced us all to the audience, and I was always 'That old haggis who speaks a foreign language – she hasn't learned to speak English yet.' He took the mickey out of the announcer, out of Paul Fenhoulet, the orchestra leader, out of Tom Ronald, the producer, until the audience felt they were at a party and were ready to lap up everything which came their way.

But one stunt he had to stop was his mock striptease. I never realized until the night he did that that it was possible to laugh to the point of sheer exhaustion. He had turned to the orchestra and asked them to play 'A Pretty Girl is Like a Melody', which apparently was the tune to which the famous Gypsy Rose Lee did her striptease. The boys in the band entered into the spirit of the thing, and played as requested, most beguilingly. Ben pranced from one end of the stage to the other, glancing coquettishly over his shoulder at the audience. Like me, I don't suppose they'd ever seen a real striptease but there was no mistaking his antics. First he pulled one shoulder of his jacket aside, then as the violins throbbed he covered the exposed shirt again. A ripple of laughter went through the hall. Then the other shoulder was revealed, and mincingly covered up. Then a button of the coat undone, then another, with a drum-roll as each button popped.

The place was in an uproar and I was clutching my sides.

Bebe, who no doubt had seen him perform this party piece before, was intent on studying her script.

The rest of the cast was in hysterics, like me.

The jacket came off and was tossed with leering abandon to the floor.

As the harp rippled seductively, he placed a finger under his braces and pinged it softly. Yells from the audience. Then to another musical *glissando*, the other brace was pinged.

When both braces were dropped to his waist you might have heard the laughter at the top of Big Ben!

At this point, he jerked both hips to the drum-roll which finished the performance, and strolled off to a storm of applause.

But he had exhausted all of us.

We couldn't move.

Worse, the audience had used up their strength and their laughter, and *nothing* we said from that precious script could raise a giggle. The show was as flat as a pancake.

We all learned our lesson that night, and the striptease was never repeated.

It was a pity about the script, for it was a specially strong one, but I wouldn't have missed Ben's striptease for anything.

2

Ben had a philosophy, which he passed on to me: 'Activity breeds activity.' By Jove, I proved the truth of this when I joined *Life with the Lyons*. I'd no sooner settled in happily to being Aggie than Charlie Chester decided he'd like me to be his secretary, Bubbles, in his weekly comedy series. The producer was Leslie Bridgmont, who had given me my very first London broadcast, and also in the cast was my old *ITMA* friend Deryck Guyler, so I was on friendly familiar territory. I was to discover that once one was in Light Entertainment it was almost like being in a private club, for one met the same people in all sorts of shows, and I was secretly elated by their acceptance of me as one of themselves.

How could they know that in my heart of hearts I felt it was all a dream, and that any minute I'd wake up? I was still starstruck, and couldn't quite believe it when newspapers and magazines asked for interviews, and described me as 'rising star, Molly Weir'. Rising stars surely didn't become so excited as I did when anybody offered them a part? How could the word 'star' apply to anyone like me who almost fainted on being introduced to Kenneth Horne and Stinker Murdoch? Wouldn't a real star be far more blasé, take it all much more as a matter of course and not have this feeling that the bubble would surely burst at any moment, and all illusions be shattered?

But if it *was* all going to be as illusory as a shooting star then I determined to enjoy every brief moment of it. *The Charlie Chester Show* was different as chalk from cheese from *Life with the Lyons*. Charlie could draft and write his half-hour show on the train between Manchester and London, and *he* was the first one in the queue for the cup that cheers before we so much as glanced at the script. He had a nice knockabout sense of comedy, and never lost a moment's sleep over the fact that he had to produce a little topical piece of doggerel every single week. We were all roped in for this chore, and for me it was back to my schooldays when I used to make up the verses for the Christmas cards and the birthday greetings, and it was the greatest thrill to hear some of my 'gems' for the Chester show chanted later that evening.

The one everybody remembered, and the most succinct, had been among the first he devised, and it was a wartime one. The cast were supposed to be engaged in jungle warfare, and to throbbing drums they had chanted:

> '*Down in the jungle,*
> *Living in a tent,*
> *Better than a pre-fab –*
> *No rent!*'

Nobody ever bettered that one.

We scanned the newspapers for topical ideas, and chewed the ends of our pencils, as we perched on the seats in the Paris cinema, where we now also did the Lyons' show, and the minutes ticked past as we scribbled, chanted aloud to see what reactions we'd get, crossed the verse out and started again.

Some of the cast, of course, didn't bother, declaring that the whole thing was beyond their skills. I'd never admit that a single thing was beyond me, apart from maybe turning cartwheels or singing in opera, and I was elated when I had my first bit of doggerel accepted and included in that evenings's show.

It was during one of our eternal fuel crises, and we'd just that day lost the Ashes in Australia. So Weir came up with:

> 'Another fuel crisis,
> And cricket's in a state.
> The only ashes we will get
> Are in the grate!'

Leslie Bridgmont was highly amused that a mere female, with no interest in cricket whatsoever, could come up with such a male joke. And the audience, sitting in a half-heated theatre that evening, roared their appreciation that we could find humour in our miseries. I felt, somewhat immodestly, that Churchill might have approved!

Another troubled situation found my muse successful again. The country was flooded with torrential rains and the newspapers were filled with pictures showing fields awash and cars up to their axles in swirling water. There were fierce arguments in Parliament over the oil situation, because of some crisis with Persia over fuel supplies.

So I cleared my throat after a bit of scribbling that afternoon, and intoned:

> 'Parliament's a mess again,
> Tempers on the boil.
> And on the troubled waters —
> Persian oil!'

Charlie and Leslie were delighted. The audiences were now beginning to wait with high expectancy for our doggerel summarizing of some topical news, and I was thoroughly enjoying my popularity as unpaid Poetess Laureate! The audience that evening again shouted their approval, and punctuated that part of the show with enthusiastic applause.

I had only one more success in this field, but it was a nice feminine one and I liked it best of all. I had read in that morning's paper that Hedy Lamarr was being married for the sixth time. This news was followed by the bewildering item that she was auctioning her entire wardrobe! I jotted down my doggerel immediately, and when we had had our usual read-through of the script and were about to tackle the topical verse, I said, 'I think I've got one. Would you like to hear it before we try anything else?'

'Well,' said Leslie, 'there's confidence if you like.'

Charlie grinned good-naturedly. 'Whose show is this, anyway?' he asked, with a wink all round. I blushed in confused embarrassment. I had only been trying to save everyone's time, for of course if they liked my verse, then we could go on with the next part of our rehearsal without chewing over any other ideas.

'Go on, Molly,' the others encouraged. 'Spit it out and we can get on with the script.'

Now that I had everyone's attention, confidence in my epic evaporated. Why did I allow my enthusiasm to run away with me? Why couldn't I just sit back quietly and let other people make fools of themselves if they wanted to, instead of setting myself up to be shot down? Och well, if they didn't like my verse, it wasn't the end of the world, I told myself. So with my head bent over my script I chanted:

> 'Hedy's getting wed again,
> Flogging all her clothes.
> Song for wedding number six —
> "Only a rose"!'

Charlie slapped me on the back. 'That's it, Molly,' he said. 'That is definitely it.' The audience too approved, and greeted my third and last contribution with generous laughter and applause. It wasn't the most hilarious joke in the world, but it was topical, and it was mine!

As well as Deryck Guyler and myself, we had Len Martyn who deafened me one night in the opening chorus when we came to the line 'Sound that horn' by sounding the horn right in my ear. I didn't hear a single cue for at least three minutes afterwards, and thought he'd injured my eardrums for life! I rounded on him with such fury at the end of the show that he never again attempted to play a practical joke on me. With my mother's tragic deafness a constant example of the misery suffered by those with poor hearing, he couldn't have offended me more or sabotaged a radio performance more effectively when it was vital to hear every cue instantly. It had been sheer thoughtlessness, of course, not deliberate malice, and my anger evaporated when I saw how contrite he was.

Fred Ferrari was the singer, with his own solo each week, and Edna Fryer, a newcomer to radio, was brilliant as Charlie's foil. One of the characters she played was truly up to *ITMA* standards, catchphrase and all. She was supposed to be mad about books, and Charlie ended each little sketch with her by saying, 'Well, reading again are you? I hope you won't read in bed.' 'Oh yes,' she would say fervently, 'I *love* reading in bed. I always sez to myself, I sez, Get you between them sheets, and read you between them lines.' This catchphrase caught on immediately, and was echoed all round the country.

Kenny Morris, as well as taking part in the sketches, was a brilliant pianist who also contributed musical items. Sandy and I were absolutely mesmerized when we first met him at Charlie's house at the Christmas party which introduced us to each other before the start of the series. We saw him take a tiny slip of paper about the size of a postcard from his pocket, and place it on the music stand of the piano. There were about half a dozen doh-ray-mees and a few words written down, and we fully expected him to pick them out with one finger.

Instead, with a rippling *glissando*, he launched into 'Night on a Bare Mountain' with all the verve and expertise of a performer at the Festival Hall. He told us later he couldn't read a note of music, was entirely self-taught, but loved the pianoforte with a deep and abiding passion. He was Welsh, and musical to the very tips of his talented fingers.

As well as finding a piece of doggerel each week for the Chester show, we also had to learn a new song, written specially by Charlie on each occasion. Incidentally, I was always amazed that Charlie took his singing voice and his musical skills so much for granted, and valued them so much less than his comedy writing. In my eyes it should have been the other way round, for I felt the gift of music came straight from heaven.

Without a piano at home to check the correct key and tune of a brand-new song every week I became very worried, for we only sang the piece together on the day of the show and there was no time to make mistakes! I talked it over with Sandy, and he, knowing how conscientious I am, agreed that now that I had two series running concurrently and could afford a major purchase like this, it would be a good idea to have our own piano. He suggested I ask Kenny Morris what he would recommend, and, thanks to my asking Kenny's help over this purchase, I had a hilarious demonstration of the power of music which was pure Hollywood.

We didn't have much space in our small living room, and I thought a mini-piano might be the best buy. Kenny arranged to take me up to an Oxford Street shop during the lunch-hour to see what was on offer in the way of a good second-hand piano. New instruments were very expensive at that time, and he assured me he knew the manager and would get the best deal possible. He would test it out and make sure I wasn't palmed off with a dud.

The shop was fairly empty when Kenny sat down and played a little Strauss waltz on a mini-piano whose size I'd judged to be just right for our small room. Kenny dismissed it as no good. No resonance. A nice ornament, yes, but not a true musical instrument as he knew it. A piano wasn't a piece of furniture to be fitted into an available space, he told me. It was a source of music and joy, and space would have to be made to receive it, even if the whole room had to be changed round to accommodate it!

I hadn't realized what I was letting myself in for.

How could he know I came from a background where a lovely polished mahogany case was the first requirement of any piano? The musical part of it we took for granted.

He had swooped over to an upright, on the whispered advice of his friend the manager, and I was dismayed to observe that if this was to be mine, it would have to go into the lounge, and we'd have to move the sideboard, and that would mean shifting the wee table, which meant the standard lamp would have to go elsewhere. While I was doing all this 'flitting' in my mind Kenny was rippling up and down the keyboard.

Then, throwing back his head, he plunged, full *fortissimo*, into the 'Warsaw Concerto'. It was like a Judy Garland musical. Passers-by stopped, gazed into the shop, then came in, lured by the magic of the music. Desultory would-be purchasers, already inside the shop gathered round the piano. Kenny played on, oblivious. From the 'Warsaw Concerto' he went into Brahms, then Beethoven's Fifth, completely absorbed in the music and ignorant of the rapt audience which filled the shop. As he let the last note echo away like a sigh, the whole shop broke into spontaneous applause. I was absolutely thrilled. Hollywood hadn't exaggerated one little bit in those Garland musicals. It could all happen. I knew it could, for I had just seen it.

We took that piano, of course. There was no question of any other. It had the seal of approval from Kenny, the manager and an audience of clerks, typists, and shoppers, who now went on their way happier for having taken part in this unexpected lunchtime concert.

I have it still. Kenny himself died tragically young, but every time I look at the piano, which still takes up far too much room in our present dining room, I see again his dark head and his dreamy eyes and, above all, his strong, clever fingers drawing music which had in it a sort of magic, and which, on one memorable day, drew the crowds like a Pied Piper from the busy pavements of Oxford Street.

It was in the Chester show that I first met Stinker Murdoch and Kenneth Horne. As I emerged from the dressing room where I'd changed into my short dark red velvet dress to look my best for the audience, there were the famous pair strolling towards the stage, scripts in hand. They were to be our guests for that evening. When Deryck Guyler introduced me, Stinker took my hands, held me at arm's length, and after a long examination said in those famous light humorous tones, 'You look exactly as I hoped you would look.' Deryck laughed and said, 'Well, that just about equals Beverley Nichols' remark to the lady to whom he said, "Come into the garden and let my roses see you." ' I absolutely agreed with Deryck, although I couldn't utter a word. I was fair dazzled, and Stinker had made a fan for life!

He and Kenneth later brought the house down with one of their famous musical numbers, where they took a well-known aria or overture and put fast and completely inappropriate words to it, like a tongue-twister. I remember the one they did that evening began:

> 'Sticky Bath buns are four for elevenpence,
> Caraway seeds are seven for sevenpence',

and I was fascinated to find the same skill and fast delivery which were characteristic of Tommy Handley, and the same absorption with words.

Joan Harben told me that once when she was on a long journey by car with them, Kenneth and Stinker whiled away the tedium by having a competition to see who could invent the funniest proper names using ordinary dictionary words. 'Will Fulness,' said Kenneth. 'Al Bum,' responded Stinker. 'Mag Nanimous?' queried Kenneth. 'Ben Umb,' came the response. But Joan said the game was unquestionably won when Kenneth sent them into gales of laughter with his 'Chas Titybelt.' Nobody could top that!

It was in the Chester show too that I started taking part in live TV revue. We did an hour's show every Saturday night for six weeks – live – not recorded as most shows are today, and there were so many songs, dances, sketches, and solo items following one another in rapid succession that for the first time in my life I had actually to pin the running order of the show on my dressing room mirror, or I'd never have known which clothes to leap into as I finished each item.

We worked on the Saturday from nine o'clock in the morning, and almost the most terrifying part of it for me was the fact that Eric Robinson, that lovably expert musical director and conductor, was in *another studio* listening to us on headphones and I wasn't able to watch for the beat! I've always been one to watch the conductor's baton and to *look* at the musician or musicians who come in on the first note, and to have to depend entirely on my ears in the midst of such tumult had me shaking with nerves that I'd ruin everything by belting out the opening a split second before everybody else, or roar out a wrong note! It never happened, but that didn't stop me working myself into a lather of fear each Saturday that this might just be the night when it would. I fully endorse the wisdom of the man who said, 'Most of the great worries from which I have suffered during my lifetime never happened.'

We went over some of the sketches so often, and we jumped back and forth over the items so many times out of sequence, that there were many Saturdays when I couldn't decide whether we were going through yet another rehearsal or if we were actually doing the show. Only the little red flickering light on top of the camera, indicating that it was alive, disciplined me always to duck round it, just in case we were on vision and I'd be in full view of the watching audience at home as I dashed to change costume. I wasn't the only one, I was glad to note, who felt this sense of confusion. Many a time as I leaped into the next outfit a voice would call over, 'Is this a rehearsal, or have we started in earnest?'

We may have died a thousand deaths with the urgency and speed of the whole thing, but the audiences loved it, and they particularly liked seeing us doing such a wide variety of characters.

Charlie Chester delighted me, as well as taking my breath away, with his flattering assumption that I could do anything. I played everything from Salvation Army lass to nagging housewife. I sang, and I danced, and I mimed. One script actually called upon me to do an impersonation of Shirley Temple. Charlie hadn't even bothered to ask me if I could do such a thing – he simply took it for granted that I could. Now I hadn't actually seen Shirley Temple's films, only clips used for the trailers, but I did know she was an excellent little dancer, and that she had a very special quality of voice. I also was aware that probably everybody in the country knew her voice and delivery much, much better than I did, and would be highly critical of any impersonation.

We got the clothes right. Little pink frilly dress, white socks and black shoes, and a wig of tumbled curls. Then I went to Broadcasting House and to Aeolian Hall and got out their only available records to try to get the voice accurately. Unfortunately the single recording they had at that time was an LP of the stars at some charity concert, and there was the merest snippet of Shirley singing part of the chorus of 'On the Good Ship *Lollipop*'. I listened to that over and over again, until I was sure the needle would cut right through the groove, but I realized I was right to be so fussy, for this was not just a little childish voice, it was of a very special type, with a throaty gurgle and a phrasing which was hers alone.

I worked on it. I badgered those who had seen her films to confirm that her little dance was the sort of 'time step' we learn in tap dancing, and in the end I was reasonably satisfied that I had got as close to the little child star as I could. It was only a tiny item in the hour-long show, but it was as perfect as I could make it. Nobody asked me to go to all this trouble, but I love a challenge, and I always sought perfection if it was humanly possible to achieve it.

Edna Fryer went into hysterics when she saw me in the costume, especially my legs in those socks and shoes. I've always had strong muscular legs with all the walking, dancing and cycling I've done, and they were hardly a replica of the chubby babyish limbs of the six-year-old I was supposed to be imitating. But all that was forgotten as I went into 'On the Good Ship *Lollipop*' in the throaty tones of the little star, and then leaped into her dance. It was received with warm laughter and generous applause, and even had a little notice all to itself from the critics afterwards. This Chester revue was certainly a marvellous 'stretching' exercise for me, and was allowing me to try things I'd never have had the nerve to suggest for myself.

During that particular year when I was doing both the Lyons' show and *The Charlie Chester Show*, plus the Chester TV series, everybody else seemed to want my Scottish voice in their shows too. I found myself playing Bob's girl friend in *Mrs Dale's Diary* for a brief week or so before the show broke for their summer holidays. I played an assortment of characters for my beloved *Children's Hour*, the wee 'stute fish in *How the Whale got its Throat*, a jumping bean in a fairy-tale, a nannie transformed into a mouse for *Rapunzel*, not to mention a French governess in *Jennings at School*, and a similar part in *The Bell Family* by Noel Streatfeild. May Jenkin was highly amused when I played the wee mouse, for she had thought she'd have to find a mechanical device to achieve the right sound of a mouse's squeak. After trying various ideas, with the sound engineer drawing his fingers down a piece of plastic, rubbing two pieces of wood together, scraping a pencil against a slate, I meekly asked if I could try it with my voice.

May pressed the key from the control room. 'Go ahead if you think you can do it, Molly,' she said doubtfully. I gave three wee squeaks, like the time-pips, and there was a gurgle over the control room mike. 'You sound *exactly* like the nicest wee Scots mouse imaginable,' she said. 'Just make your own noises then, right through the script.'

Diana Maddox, who played Rapunzel, said to me, 'Molly, you are the *sweetest* wee mouse. I can see you, from the tip of your quivering nose to the end of your velvety tail, and I could *eat* you all up!' Not for nothing had I been trained by Moultrie Kelsall to find all sorts of solutions in my own throat, from consumptive coughs to three-hundred-year-old Peerimen!

I loved that part of the wee mouse, and it made a challenging 'double' to be restored to my former self as an aged nannie, and go from squeak to kindly old lady in a split second.

David Davis wrote the most enchanting music to accompany those tales for the children, and I often thought how subtly juvenile musical tastes were being educated to appreciate only the best through listening to *Children's Hour*.

Speaking of music, one memory stands out very strongly. It was the day we were recording an episode of *Rebecca of Sunnybrook Farm* and we'd had a tea-break. Lewis Stringer, who played the romantic lead in the story, had dashed out to collect a record he had ordered, and when he returned to the studio he begged Josephine Plummer, our much-beloved producer, to be allowed to play it so that we could all hear a new sound and a new voice which he was sure was going to rocket into the Top Ten immediately. Jo set it on the turntable and we all sat round, scripts in hand, to listen.

Out poured the most incomprehensible jumble of sounds I'd ever heard. I couldn't make out a word, but the voice was infectiously lively, the music toe-tapping, and the whole thing so far removed from the dreamy 'I'll see you again' type of song which I associated with records that I might have been listening to something from another planet. That was the first reaction I had to skiffle. The voice was that of Tommy Steele and the song was 'Singin' the Blues'.

We all gazed at Lewis's rapt face and tried to look enthusiastic. We looked at one another and raised our eyebrows. The record ended. 'Well, shall we get on with the rehearsal?' said Jo. Only Lewis was aware that with this record was going to be ushered in a whole new concept of popular music, that skiffle would be followed by rock and roll, and the Beatles, and soul music, and that equally startling social changes would follow. We others suspected nothing. And yet I wonder. Perhaps I had a dim feeling that this moment was significant, else why should I remember it so vividly down through the years?

The Schools' Department used me too, and my circle of radio colleagues was ever widening, as was my acquaintance with new producers. With Jimmy McKechnie I read poetry on the Third Programme, and had to get my tongue round the unfamiliar sounds of Lallans. For David Thompson I had to be a seal in a lovely programme about the West Highlands, where almost all the rest of the cast spoke true beautiful Gaelic, and had travelled down from the Hebrides for the show. I loved the Features Department almost as much as *Children's Hour*, for the stories were vivid and real, and they were written and produced by dedicated men of true vision and enthusiasm: D. G. Bridson, Joe Burroughs, Tom Waldron and many others whose names are now known only in the archives.

There was one week, indeed, when my man said the *Radio Times* read like 'Molly Weir's Diary'. There I was in *Woman's Hour*, schools, features, *Life with the Lyons*, the Chester show, *Children's Hour*, and Third Programme poetry. When the tide is running with you like this, how hard it is to visualize a time when the phone will remain silent, and you will be left high and dry, as unwanted as a month-old fish!

But I was able to share a bit of my luck with an out-of-work actor whom I'd met when I went for a film audition one afternoon. He told me he was married to a nurse and was ashamed to feel she was keeping him, for he simply couldn't find enough work in show business to justify staying in expensive London much longer. 'Give me your name and telephone number,' I told him, 'for I'm often asked if I know of good Scottish actors. With me being in a regular series, producers think I know everybody who is Scots in the capital, and they come to me for names.'

Now in show business people are always promising one another they'll remember them when the right moment comes along, and somehow they either forget or they lose the piece of paper with the telephone number, or they just don't bother to pass on recommendations. So I think Jack Stewart gave me his name and number with small hopes of anything happening.

As luck would have it I was doing a feature for David Thompson the following week and after the recording he invited us all round to the Stag's Head, and he particularly asked me to come because he wanted to check up on some Scottish islands for a future documentary he was planning.

I now knew better than to refuse to go to a pub on Presbyterian principles, for I realized I could sip a tonic water without offending a soul, and I appreciated the fact that English pubs were really much more like social clubs, bearing little resemblance to the hard-drinking establishments of Glasgow.

As I sipped my tonic water a producer strolled over. 'Molly,' he began, 'do you happen to know a good Scottish actor whose face is not known to the general public? I'm starting a new police series on TV, and I want a completely unknown face to play the Scottish policeman so that he won't be identified in the public mind with any other part.'

'I have the very man,' I said with some excitement, delighted to be able to redeem my promise so quickly. I looked in my purse, found name and number and handed it over.

When I was at the Lyons' rehearsal later that week, Jack telephoned my husband and said, 'I don't know how to begin to thank Molly for what she did for me. I was on the point of packing it all in and going home when I had a call from a TV producer asking me to come along to see him. I couldn't imagine how he'd ever heard of me, and when he told me that Molly had recommended me to him I nearly disgraced myself and almost burst into tears.'

Sandy said the fellow was quite emotional on the telephone, and kept saying that people *say* they'll help, but nobody does, and that this had completely restored his faith in humanity. As well it might, mind you, for not only did he get the part, he got the whole series! A whole TV series, which established him as the perfect Scottish bobby, a part he filled with distinction for years afterwards, rising occasionally to the rank of superintendent as the script demanded, and making himself a welcome face in every drama where the law played its part. And yet, with the capriciousness of show business, I never saw him again in the flesh. We were just destined to meet that once, so that I had the opportunity of stretching out a helping hand.

In the midst of all this London activity I was still keeping in touch with Helen Pryde, and as soon as the Chester TV Saturday night shows were completed she fitted me into another *McFlannels* episode. Now I was a London artist, with no home in Glasgow, the BBC had not only to pay my fee but they had also to pay my fare and sleepers. This gave me a highly charged sense of responsibility, and I always felt I had to be nothing less than brilliant to justify all this expense! It wasn't that my fees were so starry, but even then fares more than doubled my cost to the BBC.

I remember one particular episode where Willie McFlannel is marooned on the roof of his house because I plot with giggling Bella (dear Effie Morrison) to steal his ladders. It went spendidly in rehearsal and, as I thought, in the live performance which followed.

When Howard Lockhart, our excellent and dearly loved producer, emerged from the control room I said, as I always did, 'Well, Howard, how did it go? Was it as good as in rehearsal?' I had moved away to collect my things, confidently expecting an enthusiastic 'Oh yes, it was fully up to rehearsal standard, if not better.'

Instead there was a little silence. I looked up in surprise. When I saw his gloomy expression my heart turned to lead. 'I thought you were all very "down",' he said, 'especially you, Molly – you didn't have Ivy's usual gallus attack.'

I really felt sick. All the way back to London in the sleeper I kept hearing his words to the rhythm of the wheels. 'You-were-all-very-down. Espe-cia-lly-you.' All that money spent to bring me to Glasgow, and I'd spoilt the episode. They'd never have Ivy back again, that was certain.

But, strangely enough, when the public were asked to write in and choose their favourite *McFlannels* episode, which would be repeated at their request, *that* was the episode they chose! So it was a vindication of the oft-repeated show business cliché that we are never the true judges of our own performances, for we are much too close to be impartial. Only this time it applied to our producer!

And I had lain awake all night in that blessed sleeper worrying for nothing!

3

One of the nicest things about having our own home was that we could have Miss Chree to spend part of the Christmas celebrations with us. I used to hate leaving her in the digs while I went off to Scotland or on tour, although I knew that she went out for one annual festive meal to some mysterious friends from her distant London past.

I never heard many details of how the friendship had begun, and they remained forever shadowy and distant, like figures remembered from Dickens. I could visualize without difficulty, though, the faded stuffy genteel setting, the huge meal, the heavy conversation, with Miss Chree sitting in their midst, rakish and elegant, probably an object of pity to these well-settled, respectable middle-class Londoners, although I had no doubt she was streets ahead of them in liveliness, wit and romantic appreciation of the London scene.

When I had asked her why she trailed half across London to share what sounded a most unfestive board, she had cast her eyes towards the ceiling and said, with a comical grimace, 'I couldn't hurt their feelings, dear. They are trying to be kind to poor spinster Jane.' I think too that she had so few friends that she was incapable of snapping this once-a-year tenuous link which held them together.

Indeed I only ever heard of one other friend of hers, a maiden lady like herself, the manageress of one of the shops owned by a famous dairy chain, to whose flat she took herself off on regular Saturday visits throughout the year, usually about once a month. Miss Chree never wore the welcome off anyone's mat by too frequent visiting.

I heard one dramatic tale of this never-to-be-seen lady, which taught me a valuable lesson which I tucked away safely in my mind, to be used with profit if I ever needed it in the future. A masked burglar had entered the shop late one Saturday night and had demanded the day's takings. It was only after he had left with the contents of the till in his greedy pockets that it had dawned on her that to have brought a dozen neighbours to her aid all she need have done was to have hurled a bottle or a tin through the plate-glass window. It was a safe bet too that the exploding glass would have sent the burglar rushing into the street with empty hands.

As Miss Chree said, destruction was so alien to the normal law-abiding citizen like her friend that it was only when it was too late that it had occurred to her that the breaking of one of her employer's windows was nothing measured against the loss of Saturday's takings, when all the weekly bills were settled over the counter.

I never forgot that story, and I hoped that if ever I were in a similar situation I'd have the courage to sacrifice a window in the interests of administering rough justice, a good fright to a thug, and a deterrent to future criminal activities. I also told everybody I knew who worked in a shop to have a hefty jar or tin handy under the counter, ready for an inside piece of window-smashing in case of need!

Just as Miss Chree kept her friends in little separate compartments, so that we none of us ever met, she also refused to visit us if anyone else was invited. This was particularly trying at Christmas, when we also invited

Sandy's ex-RAF friend Van and his wife, who were also only in digs, for I couldn't have them at the same time as Miss Chree, and have one glorious orgy of cooking and be done with it.

Whatever day Miss Chree chose for her visit, Van and Sue had to come the day before or the day after.

I tried to coax her to come with them, but it was no good. They were longing to meet her, as indeed was everyone to whom I spoke of Miss Chree. When I would start quoting her people would say, 'You *must* bring her along to see us'; or, 'Oh, *do* ask me to tea when she's coming.' All had to be told that Miss Chree flatly refused to meet any of them.

I think they doubted her existence and thought that I had invented her, like that invisible character Bunbury in *The Importance of Being Earnest*. In fact I know some of them did, for darling Jo Plummer, my *Children's Hour* producer, said to me one day, 'I don't believe there *is* a Miss Chree. You have made her up.'

This was after I had told Jo, with amused admiration, of Miss Chree's ingenuity in dealing with a bargain pair of shoes she had picked up at one of London's street markets. Finding them too cramped for her long elegant feet, she had simply cut the toes out. This was long before the days of peep-toe shoes, and she preceded that fashion by a good many years, and earned many a strange look as passers-by observed her toes chastely emerging from a neatly cut hole in the front of her shoes. And yet, even with such obvious signs of eccentricity, she still looked elegant, for she had a natural style which defied mere fashion, or lack of it.

Food was quite incidental to her. Friendship, companionship and good conversation were what mattered. She would have been quite content with a bowl of soup and some buttered toast for her Christmas meal, although she herself arrived laden with gifts. Knowing her tiny income, Sandy used to be appalled, but I shook my head at him warningly. I knew it was important to her to be able to bring things which were in perfect taste, and which I might not have thought to provide for the larder. She never earned more than £3 10s a week in all the years I was privileged to be her friend, but she glowed with happiness in bringing to our home the foods which were eaten in the best houses in London.

Dipping her hand into her rather battered carrier bag she would produce a tin of Romary's biscuits. She would purse her lips fastidiously, in imitation of a noble lord for whom she happened to be working just then. 'Bath Olivers,' she would say in hushed tones. 'Perfection.' Laying the tin down she would add, 'With a piece of good cheese, they are delicious. Or, of course, with a glass of wine – excellent.' She revelled in this exchange from the land of high living.

Another tin would be handed over, this time from Simmers of Aberdeen. She had somehow managed to find the biscuits in London, and again 'They were simply of the highest quality.'

Drawing out a paper bag next, she would affect a careless manner. 'I don't know if you have come across these, dear,' she would say, 'but I think they're rather good.'

While opening the bag I was aware of Sandy fidgeting in the background at this leisurely unfolding of each offering while the soup bubbled invitingly in the kitchen. I ignored his eye as I discovered half a dozen mouth-watering almond biscuits at the bottom of the bag, just as I used to find the tangerine in the toe of my Christmas stocking.

'Oh, Miss Chree,' I would say, '*where* did you find such delicious looking biscuits?'

Placing a hand on my arm, she would say, with purring satisfaction, delighted to have surprised me, 'I *thought* they might be new to you. They're *exquisite*.' Then, carelessly, like an afterthought, 'They're from that *rather* special *pâtisserie* which makes the cakes for Churchill.' I could have wept for such generosity from such a slender purse, but I knew it came from a full and loving heart, and I knew too what fun she would have derived from making that purchase in that famous shop.

On the way to the dining room, she had to stop to admire all the little treasures we had bought together in our forays through the London street markets and the Clapham antique shops, and rejoice over how 'right' they now looked in their proper setting. I dared not interrupt this exploration and minute assessment of every item by the slightest suggestion that the potatoes might be burning, or the vegetables reaching the soggy stage. Sandy kept darting into the kitchen, while this inspection took place at a snail's pace. Only the mention that the Queen's speech would be on at three o'clock would remind her that there was a meal to be eaten first, and at long last we would sit round the table together. She always declared herself 'dennered' with the soup course, put the turkey or goose or ham aside to be parcelled for taking home later, and went on to the Christmas pudding with its brandy butter or cream.

We always had to stand for the entire duration of the Queen's speech. With rapt attention Miss Chree would listen to every word. She had neither radio nor television, and this magic presence of Her Majesty in our midst moved her beyond measure. 'Beautiful,' she would whisper at the end, tears in her eyes, 'beautiful,' and she refused to be seated until the last notes of the National Anthem had faded into complete silence.

There was always a drink to hand to toast the Queen, and then we would sit in the firelight listening to the Orpheus choir singing 'All in the April Evening' and 'The

Faery Song' from *The Immortal Hour*. She and her sister had sung 'All in the April Evening' as children at school in Aberdeen, and she would be away on a tide of reminiscence of her loving mother, and of her father who grew so incensed when she dreamed and drooped over her books that he would threaten to 'put those books on the back of the fire' if she didn't stir herself to her duties. There weren't many people in London who knew Scottish ways and the braid Scots tongue, to whom she could speak so freely and emotionally of her family, and it was a delight to listen to her conjure her close family atmosphere until we felt we were part of it, as we drowsed before the fire. Nothing had to be explained. Nothing interpreted. Only those who live permanently in a country whose ways and tongue are not their own can appreciate the freedom of expression when all spring from the same background.

They were Christmases of pure enchantment that we spent with Miss Chree, for we were all utterly at peace and in harmony with one another. Well, maybe Sandy wasn't quite so entirely content. I think he would have preferred our dear Jane to have eaten more, and to have brought fewer gifts, but I who knew her so well wouldn't have changed anything. I knew with a deep loving awareness what made her happy, and I knew she was content. We were her family for that one day, and, independent though she usually was, she gave herself up to belonging to us and relaxing completely with us for this brief pause in her working life.

At the end of the evening, for she steadfastly refused to stay overnight, her carrier bag was packed with goodies for her larder. I always liked to make sure that if unemployment had to be faced for any reason, she wouldn't have to worry over food for a week or so. Crispbread which would stay fresh was always a good standby, various cheeses which would keep and which were nourishing were added. A jar or two of my homemade jams, jellies, pickles and chutneys to add piquancy to her diet, and which I knew she enjoyed. She could make a meal of cheese and chutney at any time, and relish it, for she wasn't one for meat. Some of the special tea and coffee from our local specialist shop, a few sweets and fudge filled the odd corners and the bag was full. This had all to be done swiftly and unobtrusively, for she would never have accepted this food openly, but we both knew it was more valuable to her against possible lean times than any fancy Christmas bauble.

We then took her up to the train and saw her on her way, at the end of a perfect day, and that was the pattern of all our Christmases.

All our Christmases, that is, apart from one glorious exception when she entertained us most royally. She happened to be working for Miss Dorothy Paget, the race-horse owner, in her town house in one of London's most exclusive squares. Miss Paget, who must have been a lady of large, imaginative and generous heart, was going away for Christmas, but before leaving she made detailed arrangements for Miss Chree's festivities, and said she was to be sure to invite one or two kindred spirits round to share the festive board. So Sandy and I were duly told to present ourselves at the basement entrance at the appropriate hour, and invited to spend the rest of the day in the house, and help consume the delicious food so thoughtfully provided by our unknown benefactor. Well, unknown in the flesh that is, although we knew of her from *The Tatler*, and our newspapers.

Miss Chree was overjoyed to play lady bountiful for a change. Everything had been delivered from Fortnum and Mason, the Queen's grocers in Piccadilly, and must have cost a small fortune. If she had fed and reared the capon herself, Miss Chree couldn't have waxed more enthusiastic over this enormous fleshy bird she now lifted on to a serving dish, appropriately stuffed by Fortnum with a truffle and breadcrumb mixture. There were potato croquettes, sprouts, and bread sauce to accompany this tastiest of birds, and Sandy and I sat at a huge scrubbed kitchen table to partake of the feast, while Miss Chree, cheeks tinged bright pink from excitement and pleasure, paused in her labours by the dresser to watch us exaggeratedly drool over every mouthful. She, of course, refused to touch a thing. 'No, I'll have it later, dears,' she said. 'I'm too full of excitement to do justice to it. I'll have it when I'm alone.' We didn't press her, for we knew her well enough to know it would have choked her just then. There would be plenty of time during the rest of the Christmas holiday for her to enjoy it, while savouring in retrospect every last detail of our visit.

The capon was followed by a slice of Fortnum's Christmas pudding, well laced with brandy, and, according to Miss Chree, posted to all corners of the world where English families celebrated the Lord's birth. Their equally famous brandy butter melted enticingly on each portion, and lent aromatic accompaniment as each mouthful melted on the tongue.

Somehow we just had to find room for a piece of Fortnum's special Christmas cake, decorated and beribboned as though for a party. Miss Paget had forgotten nothing. She had even provided a bottle of wine, a piece of Stilton cheese if required, and of course coffee.

But the final touch was somehow the most endearing of all. On one of her visits to Scotland, the lady of the house had filled the boot of her car with peat, and she had instructed Miss Chree to burn peat in the fireplace on Christmas Day so that she would feel nearer to her homeland with her Scottish friends. I was moved beyond words at the tender imaginative care of this lady, and we toasted her sincerely and enthusiastically as the peat reek curled up the chimney in the little sitting room to which we'd moved at the end of the meal.

At the close of this most unusual and delightful day Miss Chree wouldn't have dreamed of betraying her mistress's trust by showing us through the front door when we were, after all, 'downstairs' guests. So we decorously ascended the basement steps from the kitchen to reach street level. It felt languorously grand to be strolling through Belgravia on such a night, having been wined and dined in one of the great London houses, even if the fine lady who provided the feast had been absent.

Sandy always said Miss Chree and I were snobs, preferring a rich setting to cash, but who could doubt that on this day of days Miss Chree was amply justified in her choice of employment, which enabled her to play hostess against a luxurious background and entertain us in a style which was pure Oscar Wilde? How could a higher wage in suburbia compete with all that? It would have been nice, of course, if wealthy employers had also paid high wages, but I had no doubt whatever that Miss Chree's life was enriched by working in such beautiful surroundings for such colourful people, far beyond the mere rewards of money.

I loved listening to the tales of Lord Dudley and of his friendship with the Prince of Wales. Or of Harold MacMillan, who had returned very late with her employer one night, and who had offered her a half-crown for having inconvenienced her by bringing her to the door after she'd gone to bed. He had apologized for having kept her employer later than had been expected, especially when they discovered the house keys had been left in another coat! Miss Chree had refused the half-crown, feeling it an honour to work in this noble household, and had been greatly impressed with the consideration shown to her by a man whose thoughts and cares were of government and the fate of nations.

She had a fine dramatic turn of phrase, and I could just see her drawing aside to let the two late-comers in, and hear her dignified refusal of a tip for doing what was no more than her duty.

But if Christmases were now marked by much longer holidays than we'd ever known at home in Scotland, New Year was still just another working day in England. We couldn't get used to my having to go in to rehearse or record on our special day, and Ben Lyon used to tease me when I rebelliously suggested we ought to arrange our recordings so that every alternate year we had New Year off, to let Sandy and me spend an occasional Hogmanay and Ne'erday in Scotland if we wanted to do so.

'You're outvoted, honey,' Ben would grin. 'You're only one Scot who keeps those heathenish customs of celebrating Hogmanay; the rest of us prefer time off at Christmas. You can't win.'

My mother could never understand that I was Ruth among the alien corn, and just *had* to fit in with the general decision to work over the New Year period. 'Can ye no' tell them everybody goes hame fur Hogmanay?' she would write to me in utter bafflement. 'I'm sure if ye tellt Bebe' (she pronounced it 'Babe') 'she'd let ye hame a' right.' To placate her, I used to ring her on New Year's Day, although I knew perfectly well that with her deafness she wouldn't understand more than one word in a dozen, but it was a delight and a thrill for her to have a call from London.

What she *could* hear over the magic wires which now linked us was laughter, and when I'd burst into giggles over her tales of a neighbour who 'wis mirawc'lus drunk' over

Hogmanay and how he had 'fallen over Mrs Bruce's cat' she would laugh happily, just to hear me laughing, and Sandy used to call from the dining room that he'd seldom heard such a waste of time and money — two females starting the year echoing one another's laughter.

It must have sounded crazy to anyone else, but what did it matter that our conversation didn't make sense? All that mattered was that she'd been wished a Happy New Year from 'oor Molly in Pinner', and after all it wasn't everybody's mother who had been able to laugh in Springburn and have the joyous sound heard hundreds of miles away, right past London!

When she visited me in Pinner later that year, she came to a recording of *Life with the Lyons*, and Ben declared he'd give her a wee bonus just to sit there and laugh so merrily in the stalls. He almost paralysed her with fright by then asking her to stand up and take a bow as Aggie's mother, and although he was a terrific leg-puller, when he saw her face go ashen, he realized it was too much, and lightly passed on to the next introduction.

We were now long past our early politeness to one another in this famous family show. It was practically impossible to think there had ever been a time when Ben had asked me with almost embarrassed humbleness if I would mind removing my charm bracelet, as its jingling when I moved my arm upset him.

It was ages before I had realized he had the most acute hearing, and that the slightest noise during rehearsal or the actual show was agony to him. That bracelet must have driven him mad. Later, of course, he dropped this correct politeness and he'd have been more likely to say, 'Okay, honey, so you got those bits of junk out of an old haggis. So we've all seen it. So now you can take 'em off.'

My small build continually intrigued him, and he'd pick

me up, race round the studio with me, and pretend to 'leather' me when he decided I'd been too cheeky. It was as well Bebe wasn't so sensitive to noise, for she'd be working away polishing the script while all this horseplay was going on, and only when my screeching got to the level where it penetrated even her concentration would she say, without raising her head, 'Leave her alone, Ben. That's enough.' That was the signal that playtime was over for the moment, and rehearsals would now start in earnest. And woe betide any of us if we deviated by so much as a hairsbreadth from the original reading, for with the Lyons the first sight of the script wasn't just a simple read-through, it was a performance. Rehearsals were really for the sole purpose of getting the mood, the feeling, the timing and the wording so expertly that no uncertainty came between actor and performance when we came before the judgment of an audience.

When that moment of truth came, we were no longer 'reading', we were living the whole comedy situation. Which of course was the secret behind the success of the series.

Nothing had been left to chance, and it was the most marvellous example of sheer dedicated professionalism in action.

They were a fascinating family, and I wasn't the only one to come in for Ben's teasing. All the others went through it too. Particularly Barbara. She was the only one of us who had gone through the Royal Academy of Dramatic Art for her professional training, and her dad never lost the slightest opportunity of reminding her how little had come of it!

If, during a broadcast, Barbara tripped over a mike-stand or a wire Ben would fling his arms out wide. 'How do you like that!' he'd appeal to all of us. 'She's the only one who saw the inside of RADA, and she's the only ham who falls for the mike!' Barbara would join in the laughter which followed, and would smartly retort, 'He's just mad because they wouldn't let him in.' A grin from Ben and the rehearsal was resumed.

Bebe's manner of doing an 'approach' or a 'fade' line was fair game for his ribbing. To do this in front of a live audience, so that they will be kept in the picture, one should start speaking several yards from the mike, keep speaking as one approaches until full voice is accomplished; similarly, move away from the mike, speaking as one recedes, until the voice is lost. Not our Bebe. She'd stand well back all right. But the moment her cue line came up, she'd dash forward at a run, and not open her mouth to say a word until she was right up to the mike. As for 'fading', she didn't even attempt this.

Ben would stop the rehearsal. Then he'd give such a perfect imitation of Bebe's 'approach' or 'fade' that we'd all be in hysterics, with 'Mommy', as he always called Bebe, giggling more than any of us. Then he would explain. 'You see what it is, kids. She can't bear it that every word isn't crystal clear and can't be heard in Australia.'

Richard had a very cool temperament and was very easy to work with, and he and I hit it off with one another from the word go. He was an adopted son and the whole family adored him. I remember one day saying to 'Bunny', Bebe's mother, 'Wasn't Richard lucky to be taken from an orphanage into such a marvellous family?' and Bunny's immediate response, 'And weren't *we* lucky to have the privilege of taking such a lovely boy into our family?'

Richard had a great sense of humour, and I often had the same difficulty about suppressing my giggles during a show that I used to have with Gordon Jackson. There were times when we simply didn't dare let our eyes meet or we'd have ruined the scene with our laughter. And yet he absolutely refused to say, 'I wish I was dead', when called upon to do so by the script, after one teenage trauma which was supposed to have devastated him. It may have been his religion, for he was a deeply committed Catholic, often serving as altar boy in his church, or it may have been superstition, but whatever the reason the line had to be changed for he just couldn't bring himself to utter such words.

I introduced Barbara to the fun and skill of doing cross-word puzzles during the long breaks which sometimes took place when the orchestra were busy with their music, and she took to them like a duck to water. In fact they became something of an obsession, and she had to be torn away from them to rehearse! Ben found crosswords a complete mystery, but to be upsides with us he started trying to make sense of the children's crossword in the *Evening News*. He was as pleased as though he'd won an Oscar when, at one-thirty a.m., sitting up in bed after a party, he actually managed to finish one, and he was all for ringing me up there and then to tell me of his triumph. Only Bebe's commonsense and a look at the clock dissuaded him!

Living as he did in a show business household, Ben wasn't too familiar with the domestic arts I constantly practised, and he was fascinated by the sight of my needles clicking away as I knitted jerseys, waistcoats, cardigans, and all manner of woolly accessories as I waited through the series for my cues to come up. I think there were times when he wasn't quite sure whether I came along to rehearse or to knit, for I did both with equal zest.

One day, as he watched me at a firescreen I'd started to embroider as a change from knitting, he suggested I ought to buy a plain white linen teacloth, have all my working colleagues autograph it in pencil or ink, and then go over the signatures in coloured embroidery. 'What a marvellous idea, Ben,' I exclaimed enthusiastically, and went straight out in the tea-break and bought one in the linen shop in Regent Street, not far from the Paris where we were rehearsing.

The Lyons' signatures were carefully inscribed on the cloth, which we stretched and held firm on the stage of the Paris to make a good stable surface for writing.

Everywhere I went afterwards I carried the cloth with me, and it grew grubbier and grubbier as it was whipped out in the various canteens where I bumped into fellow actors, and cups and saucers were pushed aside to allow signatures to be written clearly and easily.

When there wasn't another inch of space it was such a unique record of all the famous and great people, and the little lesser lights of show business like myself, that I didn't dare risk losing such a precious memento to some star-struck laundry assistant. And, although I'm no expert, I washed and lightly starched it myself, terrified the ink under the signatures would run, or I wouldn't be able to get all the dirt out, and it would be a mess.

When I smelt the hot starch mixture, I was wafted back to the laundry classes at school, and I could hear again the teacher say to me, 'You'll never make a washerwoman, Molly.' Well, maybe not, but the cloth washed and ironed beautifully, and the BBC in Glasgow featured it in their TV programme during the fiftieth anniversary celebrations in 1973. The camera zoomed in to show Bebe's signature, with the famous little hat which was her trade mark drawn underneath. It then moved on to a signature nearby, which was a wee bit of a cheat, for I hadn't actually ever *worked* with him. Still I *had* bumped into him outside the Paris on my way to rehearsals, and I had dared to whip the cloth from my bag and thrust it under his nose, for who could resist obtaining the signature of the one and only Charlie Chaplin? I really shook with excitement that day, as I took in those neat little hands, the intense blue eyes, the shock of thick white hair, and the wide, wide smile. My mother would never believe I had actually seen her first hero, in the flesh. It was a magic moment, and it is immortalized in my autograph cloth.

I hadn't the nerve to take the cloth with me, though, on the day Ben allowed Sandy and me to go along to watch rehearsals for the Royal Film performance, which he was producing.

It was a revelation to see how patient and diplomatic Ben could be when he wished. And when I looked round the theatre and began to recognize so many famous faces – Orson Welles, Jane Russell, Peter Ustinov, John Mills, Michael Wilding, Fred McMurray, Peter Lawford, Tallulah Bankhead – I realized he would need every ounce of tact and diplomacy in his repertoire! I didn't envy him his job.

It was hopeless to expect stars of that calibre to 'jump to it', and it must have been agony for them too, for they each had a reputation to maintain – and about five minutes to do it in!

Poor Ben was the one who had to arrange the programme, work out a pretty rigid timetable, and keep them all happy! A nice trick, if you can do it!

Sandy and I were quite mesmerized sitting there in the stalls, seeing such a parade of internationally famous stars wandering on and off the stage, and finding them so quiet and understated in their ordinary clothes. Only Tallulah Bankhead sent off sparks of sheer magnetism, for she was much more used to live theatre than most of the others. There was a fascinating example of polite head-on collision when Ben tried to coax Orson Welles to go through his act without his partner, Lizbeth Scott, who hadn't arrived, just to get an idea of the timing.

They sat facing one another in the stalls, Ben perched on the back of a seat, Orson on the back of another one. I hoped the upholstery wouldn't collapse under the strain! 'But, Ben baby,' Welles was saying, 'I can't do it without a partner – that routine has to be worked out together.'

'Sure, Orson,' Ben soothed him, 'we know how it is. But I have to get an idea for my overall timing.'

'Well, Ben baby,' Orson said, not meeting his eyes, 'I think we'll just have to wait till Lizbeth gets here.'

Impasse.

Sandy and I held our breaths.

With a sigh, Ben rose, patted Welles' arm, and left him.

I must say I admired Ben's control, for he was responsible after all for the entire production. But what riveted me most of all was Orson Welles calling Ben 'baby'. I wondered if big American stars used such terms of juvenile endearment to take the edge off a steely determination to refuse to do anything which in their opinion made them look merely a part of the show and not the king-pin.

Mark you, Ben seemed able to deal with the most un-nerving confrontations. I remember his telling me how he'd had to cope with a very delicate situation during the making of a big film when he was with Twentieth Century Fox. The young leading lady, beautiful and appealing as she was, had a terrible flaw which only revealed itself under the hot lights of the film set. She suffered from such pungent b.o. that it sent the rest of the cast rocking back on their heels! Somebody had to tell her, before the other actors marched off the picture in a body! Which they had threatened to do. And that somebody was Ben.

'Ben,' I gasped. 'How could you *do* it? What did you say?'

'Well, it wasn't very nice, honey,' Ben agreed. 'But I just had her come to my office, and I put it to her that either she did something about her personal hygiene, or she didn't do the picture. For we had a threatened walk-out on our hands.'

Every time afterwards when I saw that actress in a film, I visualized the mind-boggling scene, and for courage in the face of danger I reckoned Ben deserved a gold-plated Oscar of his very own.

4

Life with the Lyons was now established so firmly as a favourite radio show that tickets for the recordings were like gold-dust, just as in the old *ITMA* days. Queues would form, winding right round the Paris into the lane at the back, and we had our regulars who tried to come every week. There was a *bona-fide* fan club, run very much on American lines, and of which up till that time I'd only read about in movie magazines. They received a quota of seats weekly, they held regular meetings, wrote letters, held parties, sent us Christmas cards, remembered our birthdays, and were united solely in their adoration of the Lyon family, which now included the rest of us in the radio cast.

One problem with having such regulars in the audience was that of clothes. We weren't encouraged to be over-dressed for what was essentially a family show (although Bebe enjoyed wearing the gladdest of glad-rags), but we recognized it was both a compliment to our audiences and a refreshment to ourselves to change into something fresh for the performance.

My nature simply wouldn't allow the extravagance of a brand-new outfit every week, just to give the regulars a treat, and my modest oak wardrobe would never have held such a variety of garments. Anyway, I'm such a magpie I could never have brought myself to throw anything out, and the house would have been bursting at the seams.

It was then that I started what I later came to call my 'cashmere bank'. I had always had a passion for this most exquisite type of yarn, ever since my mother had bought me a second-hand navy cashmere jumper during the war, when I could hardly believe anything so fine in texture could combine such warmth and elegance. Every time I put it on, I almost swooned as the incredible softness of the material touched my skin, and I knew I could wear such jumpers week after week with different skirts, and not care a button that I wasn't stunning the regulars with a completely new outfit.

So, over the season, I acquired several pleated skirts, which were my 'audience' basic wardrobe. As soon as Simpson's sale was advertised, I flew to the cashmere counter, and bought myself two garments. *Two!* What impossible extravagance to hand the saleslady a soft red cardigan-type, and a pale turquoise turtleneck jumper and say, with affected casualness, 'I'll have both.' It was a pity my voice came out in an excited squeak to spoil the effect.

My mother was amazed to see me in jumper and skirt when she came to see the show. 'My, it's great how you can manage tae look so dressy in juist an ordinary jumper and skirt,' she marvelled.

'Mother,' I said in some exasperation, 'it's *not* an ordinary jumper – it's *cashmere*.' I was very disappointed she hadn't recognized the luxury yarn on sight, especially when she herself had introduced it to me with the jumper bought at the barrows. But I realized later that it was the sheer impossibility of her imagination to grasp that anybody could possibly afford to buy cashmere *brand-new* which had made her disbelieve the evidence of her own eyes. And I do believe it was my new Simpson cashmeres which convinced her I was truly a success, and moving in very exalted circles indeed!

I bought two at every sale. I'd never have been daft enough to have paid the full price, when I knew perfectly well there was a sale every summer and every January. I bought pale shades at summer sales, and dark colours at winter ones. I was even able to persuade Bebe and Barbara of the thriftiness of such canny buying. Bebe had gone into The White House in Bond Street in late December and had paid what had then seemed a fantastic sum for an embroidered cashmere jacket.

'Bebe, you didn't,' I gasped when she showed it to me, and I saw the price tag. 'You'd have got it for half price next week.' She stared at me as if I'd gone out of my mind. She'd never heard of the January sales.

When I patiently explained there was no need to pay the top price for any expensive item, so long as you arranged your needs in such a way that nothing had to be bought in a hurry, she demanded to be taken along to the very next sale at my favourite Simpsons.

I did better than that.

I took both her and Barbara to the shop the week before the sale, and showed them all the prices.

Then on the first day of the sale, which luckily happened to be a rehearsal day for us so we could all meet in town, we plunged into the fray at the cashmere counter and they were staggered to find prices slashed in half!

The staff were almost hysterical at the sight of Bebe and her daughter, plus Aggie, diving through the boxes with all the enthusiasm of old-established bargain hunters, but they had the good sense to wait until we'd collected our chosen beauties from the cashmeres on offer before they asked for our autographs!

Always after that Bebe would say to me, at any time of the year, 'Aggie, when is the next sale? I need another sweater.' She could never remember July and January were the months. And if she had to buy anything pricey outside sale times, she felt so guilty about her lack of foresight she apologized to me!

But I think it was my horror over any waste of food which changed their attitude almost more than their sales shopping. We used to dine together in the canteen, but not always at the same table. One day when we happened to find half a dozen vacant chairs together we all sat down to eat round one big table. I noticed Ben had pushed his tomato aside.

'Are you not going to eat that, Ben?' I asked.

He looked up, startled. 'No, why? Do you want it, honey?'

'Yes,' I said, scooping it smartly from his plate. 'It's criminal to waste any food, after all the shortages we knew in the war. And there are starving Europeans whose hunger we insult if we waste anything.'

There was a stunned silence. I don't think it had ever occurred to them to reason like this. Americans never knew the food shortages we knew for so many years of food rationing in Britain. In two minutes everybody was offering all unwanted items from his plate. Bebe took Barbara's beans. Richard had Bebe's onion. Ben had Horace's mushrooms. And this was to be the pattern for all our future eating. Not a morsel went unclaimed, and nobody put fork to mouth until the general barter was over!

Even more hilarious was the day we went for tea after a Saturday afternoon rehearsal. We had collected a plate of pricey Danish pastries with our teas, and Richard, in generous mood, had paid for the lot. (In the programme he was always depicted as a tight-wad, like Jack Benny, and constantly offset his radio image by such generous gestures.) As we rose to go, there were two luscious pastries left on the plate. Barbara and Doris Rogers (Florrie) were both on their diet yet again, and had virtuously refused to be tempted, so their pastries remained untouched.

'You're not leaving those!' I exclaimed to Richard. 'They're yours. You paid for them.'

'I don't want them,' said Richard. 'I'm going to a movie.'

'Right,' I said. 'They're not going to get the chance to throw out such lovely pastries – I'll just take them home to Sandy.' And I wrapped them in my paper napkin.

Needless to say, forever afterwards, in a similar situation, all the leftover food was enthusiastically collected, not only from our own table, but from all the nearby tables, and piled into paper napkins while Ben or Richard busily explained to the startled staff and customers, 'Molly's just taking all this food home to Sandy – she's scared you'll try to sell it again!'

Everybody took it in good part, accepting it all as part of this much-loved scatterbrained family's life-style. And of course perpetuating the myth of the canny Scot!

Sandy was mad when I told him, and decided I was definitely becoming even more eccentric than Miss Chree! Actually it was Miss Chree who taught me this economy, for on the few occasions when I took her out to tea in town she was always far too excited by the occasion to eat what we'd selected from the counter, and wrapped it up to take home with her, to eat later when her mood was calmer. 'We've paid for it, dear, so it's ours,' she would say, ignoring amused or embarrassed glances from anyone who happened to be looking our way, or sharing our table. I've never been slow to follow a good example!

The general public really believed I worked for the Lyons. They were convinced they were simply eavesdropping on a normal evening or afternoon in the Lyons' household. I remember once being asked for directions by two little old ladies near Leicester Square, and the moment they heard my voice they recognized me as Aggie. They were thrilled to the marrow. 'How are the family, dear?' they asked, and then went on anxiously, 'Do you think Master Richard eats enough? He's looking very thin these days. See if you can get him to take an egg custard, and lots of milk. It's very good for him.'

We were joined by two teenagers, who had also recognized my voice, and I fully expected them to laugh derisively at the old ladies for imagining I was really part of the Lyons' household. To my amazement, one of them said, 'I'll bet Barbara won't eat all them Scotch pancakes and scones you bake, for she'll be watching her figure.'

I hadn't the heart to disillusion any of them, and meekly agreed to pass on all their messages when I was serving the dinner that night!

The Lyons themselves consulted me about food, just as though I were on the domestic staff. Rehearsals would come to a halt while Ben would demand tips for getting his roast potatoes really brown, and Barbara would suddenly remember I hadn't given her that recipe for cooking scallops in cheese sauce I'd promised.

Richard and Tom, the producer, would join in the discussion, for they all had decided views on food, and meantime the others got on with their crosswords in a corner of the studio or seized the opportunity to have another cup of tea.

Bebe, of course, was far too busy cooking up ideas for improving the script to lend an ear to such diversions, and she scribbled industriously, oblivious to the cookery class being held not two yards from her! I don't think she'd ever have remembered to eat if Ben hadn't done all the ordering and arranging of the meals. I was most intrigued by this reversal of the usual husband and wife rôles, and exchanged many a wee culinary tip with Ben as he rang home and advised the kitchen how many would be coming for dinner, what they'd like to eat and what time they'd like to dine.

Richard and Barbara were sharing a flat now, but they often joined their parents for a meal after rehearsals.

Barbara's engagement ring still dazzled me with its size and sparkle, and I was fascinated by the ease with which her fiancé, George Getty, could fly from all corners of the globe to come to the Paris to watch the recordings. He had a sort of roving commission to keep an eye on his millionaire father's interests all over the world, and he had a constant tan as though he'd never spent five minutes indoors.

A tall, quiet, handsome American was George, and I thought they made a dream couple. I was thrilled to realize he had flown in from South America to have a few hours with Barbara, although he thought no more of this journey than I would of going up to Glasgow.

And then the whole romance collapsed. Barbara decided she couldn't, she simply couldn't go to live in America. She was now badly bitten by the show-business bug and wanted to see how far she could get in her career. She had started singing the occasional ballad in the show, and had all sorts of plans and dreams for going on as a musical comedy star or a solo singer. She'd have had to put such plans behind her if she married George, for not only did he want her to live in America, he'd expect her to be by his side as wife and hostess when he entertained as lavishly as his position demanded, coming as he did from the top four hundred of Boston society.

It must have been a terrible decision to make.

But in the end George lost and went back to America alone, and we never saw him again. I grieved for him, and hoped Barbara had made a wise choice.

Nobody I knew in Springburn would have broken an

engagement, for fear of having to hand back the only diamond they'd ever possess. Small enough in most cases to require a magnifying glass to see properly, but a diamond just the same.

When I asked Barbara, with great sympathy, how she'd felt in having to hand back that blinding knuckleduster, I was staggered to learn that George had refused to take it back! She'd been allowed to keep it! Now I really *did* believe he might be a millionaire in his own right, to be able to afford to make such a generous gesture.

You will appreciate I am neither exaggerating the ring's quality or size when I tell you that much later, when Barbara visited America, she was able to trade in that ring for a mink coat, full length, *and* get change back!

I had a fur coat myself by this time – I was definitely going up in the world! – but not mink, needless to say. I'd seen an advertisement in the *Evening News* offering a 'practically new' dyed squirrel coat, small size, at a price well within my reach now that I was doing a regular show. Sandy thought it was a good idea to have a look at it, for the winters were much colder in the London area than we'd believed possible, and now that I was so identified with the Lyons I was constantly having to make personal appearances with them, and had to look reasonably prosperous! It was nice to have a good reason for both comfort and swank!

The address was in a part of London quite unknown to me, and I climbed a dark stairway where the fog lingered and stung the nostrils. I was suddenly reminded of the wee dressmaker in Springburn, and that far-off night when my mother and I had stumbled through the fog, and I'd disgraced myself by laughing down the wee wifie's ear-trumpet with sheer nerves.* How I wished my mother were

* *Best Foot Forward.*

with me now, with her good commonsense, and clear values, so that we could have had a rare argument to stop me feeling so nervous.

The coat they showed me was brand-new. It had obviously never been worn, for the small cut-off snippets of fur were still in the pockets as I thrust my hands down to admire the effect before the long mirror. The mirror was fly-spotted, and the light so dim I had to peer through the murk and wisps of fog which clung everywhere, but as I'd never seen myself in a full-length fur coat before, I had to admit it looked most opulent.

I felt uneasy. I wanted to ask why the coat was so new but I couldn't find the words. Some deep instinct told me it wasn't stolen, or I'd have run a mile from the place. But I had the distinct impression that some sort of dodge was being practised. They were probably avoiding the tax on new garments by advertising coats as 'almost new' and selling them from a private house one at a time, but they weren't second-hand at all. I felt let down, for of course what I was after was somebody's magnificent silky coat, hardly worn, at a bargain price! Not a new coat, specially run up for people like me who couldn't afford top prices in the shops.

It might not even be good quality fur. In this light, who could tell?

I'd like to have run from the house as I had run from the wee dressmaker's all those years ago, but I had neither the wit nor the sophistication to do so. I had no proper excuse either, for the coat, whatever its quality, fitted like a glove. It wasn't so silky or shiny as I'd imagined, but maybe it was the poor light. Still, at £75 it was a good deal less than the price of similar coats in the shops.

I took it, and I wore it for the first time to the big charity show we did shortly afterwards in the Coliseum. There wasn't a cloth coat to be seen in the dressing room, and I was so glad I'd plunged a precious £75 on this symbol of success! Especially when Petula Clark came in at the end of her act to claim her own brand-new squirrel coat from the pile lying on the chairs, and picked up mine by mistake!

'Hey, Petula,' I cried. 'That's my coat, and it's brand-new. It's the first time I've worn it.'

'So is mine,' she said, rummaging furiously among the furs (you'd have thought they were three a penny, there were so many). 'Ah, here it is,' she shouted triumphantly, holding up a coat which was practically the twin of my own for style, but which had the silky rippling gloss which mine had not. I wondered if she had bought hers in a real shop. I wished I had done so. I just couldn't rid myself of the uneasy feeling that I'd been taken in by a bit of sharp practice. Seeing my coat beside Petula's, I realized I had been right to suspect its quality. I never really enjoyed wearing it after that. In the end I sold it to another actress for £20.

'Aye,' my mother said when I told her. 'Toffs are careless. They saw you coming.'

It was a bitter and an expensive lesson, and it was the last time I ignored that infallible guide which has always sensed unease long before my head has, that organ implicitly trusted by the Chinese philosopher, Lin Yu Tang, my stomach!

Joan Harben had been at the Coliseum show too, and I was startled to see how pale and fine-drawn she was. I hadn't seen her for some time, although we talked on the telephone a great deal, and I invited her to come out to Pinner one afternoon and have lunch and tea with me at home.

She brought miles and miles of white silk with her, or so it seemed to me, which she bent over assiduously all afternoon, hemming the skirt of a ballgown for her daughter.

Joan knew everything that went on in London, and her daughter was to be admitted to the new young membership of one of the most sophisticated clubs in the West End, which was now opening its lists to the younger sons and daughters of their older clientele. The membership was to be a mere guinea a year, but it was the parentage which counted!

Joan and Clive had been members for years, and they thought this was a marvellous introduction for their ewe lamb into the grown-up world, where she'd meet people of her own kind and be absorbed effortlessly into the social swim.

How different from the wee church socials and dances of our Springburn social club, I thought, as I watched the tiny stitches. I couldn't imagine any of our mothers bothering themselves with our social launching. They just made sure we behaved ourselves and got home at a decent hour.

'This must be how it's done in high society,' I thought, and I was very touched by the delicate work Joan was putting into this glamorous gown. Like me, she'd had to work too hard for her money to throw it away on expensive shop fripperies, and nobody seeing the neat dark head bent over the silk could have guessed that here was one of the best-known names in radio practising the same economy as any prudent mother of a growing daughter.

Sandy and I were planning a holiday in Brittany on our tandem when the series broke later in the spring, and Joan, who'd been abroad many times, advised me on all the items we must take to avoid spending precious francs on the other side. Bicarbonate of soda for upset tummies. Insect repellent for bites. Plasters for blistered heels. Calamine lotion for sunburn. Oh, and a laxative, for foreign water did terrible things to your regular habits. It sounded the most off-putting list of items to ensure a happy holiday, but Joan assured me that spending money in foreign chemists was the least interesting way of parting with currency, and with a bit of luck we might not have to use any of our medicines. It was just prudent insurance.

We had cause to bless her many, many times during that adventurous holiday, when all her medicines were pressed into service.

But before the end of the radio series for that season an even greater prospect beckoned. *Life with the Lyons* was to be presented at the Hippodrome Theatre, Blackpool, for the whole of the summer season. There would be five weeks of rehearsals at the London Casino, followed by a week's rehearsal at the Hippodrome prior to the fourteen weeks' run. Jack Hulbert was to produce.

It was to be a play with music and dancing, chorus girls and boys, and the story-line was of a misunderstanding over a *femme fatale* who enslaves Richard, and whom Bebe imagines has ensnared Ben! The rest of the radio cast were to play their usual roles. We would do twice-nightly performances.

Twelve shows a week for fourteen weeks.

Now to do a variety spot twice nightly is bad enough, for it involves hanging around the theatre for about five hours. To do a complete play twice nightly sounded murder. It was. In the end it nearly killed us.

Sandy and I brought our tandem holiday forward so that I'd have had a good fortnight's exercise, ozone, and delicious food before rehearsals started. Everybody in Pinner knew us because of that tandem, for it was the only vehicle of its kind for miles. It was absolutely necessary for us to have such a machine if we were to proceed on two wheels, for I've never been able to ride a bicycle. I always blamed my mother for this lack of talent on my part, for she had been so terrified of the traffic in Springburn that she had forbidden me either to hire a bicycle for myself or have a shot on anybody else's, and so I never acquired this skill.

However, what is a handicap on a solo bike is a positive advantage on a tandem, for then the non-cyclist is not tempted to control the bike, to everyone's peril, but has merely to sit there, legs going like pistons, to drive the machine forward.

It was a marvellous way to see the country. No worries about parking. No anxiety about stopping because somebody was on one's heels. Just a leg thrown over the bike to start, and a similar jump to stop, and the bike leaned against a fence or wall while one admired a particularly entrancing piece of scenery.

We had two panniers (ex-army), one on either side of the tandem, to hold our change of clothing, one across the back to hold general items, like our medicine box, bathing things and towels, and my shoulder-bag slung round my handlebars, readily accessible to produce passports, tickets and cash. We had to ride into London the night before, to have the machine weighed at the station, and properly labelled, ticketed, and placed in readiness to go into the guard's van next day. We hated parting with it like this, in case it would lie forgotten and neglected and we'd arrive at St Malo only to discover our trusty steed had been left languishing at a London terminal. We needn't have worried. They were very used to handling bikes in those days, and there it was, looking reassuringly sturdy and willing, by the luggage lockers.

It was a marvellous holiday. It was the first time we'd taken our bike abroad and we revelled in being out in the sun and the sparkling air all day long. The only time we were indoors was to eat and to sleep, with not so much as a spot of rain to make us seek shelter. We ate at railway cafés, following the example of the ordinary French families and the workmen, for we were on a very tight budget. It was the year of the £50 restricted travel allowance, and we couldn't afford to be extravagant.

We sought little hotels or guesthouses at the back of the town, which were cheaper than those on the coast. Always the cheapest rooms were on the top floor, and we slept in every garret in Brittany, although the rooms on the lower floors were practically deserted for it was very early in the season. We kept shrugging our shoulders – well, at least *I* did, for Sandy refused to lower his dignity by any hinting – casting my eyes towards heaven regretfully, and mouthing, '*Ah, quelle restriction!*' in the fond hope of persuading proprietors to allow us to sleep in one of those lovely luxurious empty rooms on the first or second floors, but at the cheapest prices, of course. It was no good. They knew we couldn't spend more because of the travel allowance, and while no doubt they wished for our custom in future years when we could spend the earth without breaking the law, those flinty-hearted landlords weren't to be coaxed into giving us any bargains. A canny race, the French.

But it was all a tremendous experience, and we loved the sun, the sea, the picnic lunches and the quiet lanes where we buzzed along on the tandem like bees in clover. We bought French bread and butter and cold sausage, and devoured them all with enormous appetite when we came out of the sea, hunger sharpened by a morning's run from one little seaside town to the next.

On one terrible day, though, when we were unable to get milk at the farm where I'd tried to buy some, they offered to sell me instead a bottle of a pale home-made wine. They made a great point of my promising to return the bottle when we'd finished with it, and to make sure we did so, they handed it over without a cork! They'd noticed our bike, and knew we couldn't risk jogging along with an open bottle of wine – hence the absence of a cork. There was no doubt about it, the French were exhibiting the most extraordinary prudence. Well, we were thirsty, and we'd paid for it, and we couldn't carry any of it away with us, so we drank it all. It looked innocuous, and we had no suspicion of the potency of home-brewed country wine. We lay down for a few moments on the capes spread out below the trees, to enjoy a little after-lunch laze in the sun. We fell into what was undoubtedly a drunken stupor! For when we wakened it was dusk and our legs felt like lead when we staggered to our feet. We stared at one another, appalled. We had slept the entire afternoon! It was almost dinner-time, and we had *miles* to ride before we could reach the next village.

The farmer smiled slyly when I went back with the bottle, then laughed uproariously when I pointed to the bottle, gave an exaggerated little lurch and said, '*Dormir.*' I was covered with confusion at having to explain away an entire afternoon spent in his orchard when we were supposed to be on a cycling tour! As I walked down the path, I heard him tell his wife and son we had no head for such strong wine, and their laughter followed me back to where Sandy was fixing on the panniers ready for the journey along the coast.

Never again did we touch a drop of wine in the middle of the day. That home-made firewater went straight to our legs, and when we pressed down on the pedals it was like trying to propel the tandem through treacle.

Our vocabulary improved by leaps and bounds, though. We were in a part of Brittany where they saw few visitors, for we continued to avoid the more popular and pricey hotels and guesthouses on the coast, and the proprietors and landlords we dealt with had little English. So we just had to try out our school French to be understood. It was an excellent way to jog the memory, and improve the art of miming, and Sandy said it was an education in itself to watch me fix our accommodation one evening with a shrewd French landlady, when in the end I managed to beat her down a few francs for our room. He couldn't decide whose hands had worked faster, hers or mine, or whose shoulders had done more expressive, dramatic shrugging. When finally she threw up her hands and cried '*C'est juste*', and quoted the price I had stubbornly said she had originally quoted us earlier that day (she had too!), he had to hold himself back from seizing my arm, holding it aloft and declaring me the winner!

We used all Joan Harben's medicines. We suffered everything from burnt backs to blistered heels, and I had the added horror of herpes on my nose and lips, induced by the salty breezes. I've been a martyr to herpes since childhood, and in Brittany the constant exposure to sun and salt which was the natural condition of a cycling holiday, gave me the worst dose I'd had since I was a schoolgirl. It is a most painful and baffling virus, for it reacts equally to cold germs and salty sunshine, so the risk is always present whether one is engulfed with a snuffling cold or leaping in and out the briny on holiday.

It was such a shame. For I was now tanned to a glowing gold. Arms, legs and face. And nobody noticed the glory of my colouring for recoiling in horror from my scabs! They bled, and hideously stained hotel pillow-cases. They cracked and broke and spoilt my appetite for the beautiful food.

It was a mercy we weren't to appear at Blackpool right away, or I could never have applied stage make-up. By the grace of God, rehearsals for *Life with the Lyons* as a stage show were to be lengthy, and I would have five whole weeks to lose the effects of this blight and get my skin back to normal.

5

Normally I love rehearsals.

Sir John Gielgud once defined himself as an 'amateur' in the dictionary sense of the word. For, he said, the 'amateur' does what he must do in his chosen profession or hobby for sheer love of it, and the financial rewards take second place in all his calculations.

In this sense, I fall into that category too, or, as Ben would say in his American fashion, I'm a true 'ham'. I adore everything to do with acting, and for me rehearsals are exciting and fulfilling as we work out the best ways of presenting our plays and ourselves for the public's approval. Hours can be spent on finding a single move, or way of putting over a line, which will underline the comedy or the drama of a situation, and there is a wonderful feeling of teamwork as we all throw ourselves into discussions for improving the effects we strive for.

The moment I walked into the Casino on that first day I sensed a nervy unease in Ben. The company had already been working for a day or two but I'd been allowed to finish my holiday without interruption. I had expected an air of busy enthusiasm, and a swift order to get cracking with my script to catch up with the rest of them. Instead there was a sort of broody idleness. This was so unusual for the Lyons that the butterflies in my tummy whizzed and did somersaults of alarm which the ensuing weeks did nothing to calm.

Bebe was standing on stage, and a group of chorus girls squatted in a corner, talking quietly. Jack Hulbert was leaning against the footlights, hat pushed to the back of his head, eyes closed. Warning signals came from my ever-reliable stomach, for I felt a tense desperation in the glance Ben shot towards Hulbert.

'What's going on?' I whispered to Doris Rogers, who played Florrie, Ben's sparring partner in all the domestic rows. She raised her eyebrows eloquently, and glanced in Ben's direction. 'I'll tell you later,' she hissed out of the side of her mouth.

The only person unaffected by the atmosphere of doom was Diana Dors, who had been cast in the role of the *femme fatale* who ensnares Richard but whom Bebe mistakenly thinks has charmed Ben. I was astounded to find her slim as a willow and not the curvaceous sex symbol I'd been led to expect. Much prettier than her screen image, she had a fine delicate skin, intensely blue eyes, and the heavy mouth was soft and pink over nice white teeth.

'Where have you been?' she demanded to know, when I was introduced to her. 'The South of France? Gee, that's a gorgeous tan you've got.' Later she was to drive us all mad, but that first remark made me purr with pleasure for, having a naturally pale skin, my heart's desire is to acquire a golden bloom, which is only achieved after weeks of lying in the sun and much anointing with oils, but which alas vanishes at the first hint of a grey sky. While it does last, though, I want everybody who sees it to notice it and to be as impressed as I am! My mother could never understand this passion of mine for a tanned complexion, for with her own red hair and rose-leaf colouring, she thought pale skins were most enviable, and that I was out of my mind to want to disguise mine.

I had just been introduced to Diana's husband, a handsome chap sporting a dark blue blazer with heavily embroidered badge on the pocket, when Jack Hulbert stirred and we were all summoned to the upstairs bar to read through the script.

As soon as we started reading, the choreographer got busy putting the chorus girls through their steps on stage. He was a tall, lithe Negro, who had made a great success of the dances in the current American musical at Drury Lane, and the girls were obviously enchanted to work with him. I could see Hulbert's eyes straying in their direction, and I had a sneaking suspicion that this master of the old-style musical comedy dancing longed to be down there among them!

When we came to the end of our scene, not a word was uttered either in praise or criticism.

Ben's brows were like thunder.

This wasn't his way at all, and we who had worked with him so long knew it.

Ben likes direction, and he wanted every bit of help from a master of light comedy like Hulbert, to boost his confidence and bring out the best of which he was capable. Also, he hadn't done a stage play for years, and he was understandably nervous.

I didn't require Doris to underline what I'd already found out in that one morning. It was not going to be a happy production.

Perhaps part of the trouble was that Jack Hulbert and Bebe and Ben assumed different things. Hulbert, urbane, courteous, gentlemanly and altogether delightful, took it for granted, I think, that the famous Hollywood pair knew exactly the effects they wished to achieve, and didn't really need or expect personal detailed direction from him. He may possibly have felt they were tackling the performances in exactly the right way.

Bebe and Ben, on their part, were used to endless discussion and approval of every piece of business, and when they didn't get it, assumed either that Hulbert had given them up as a bad job or hesitated to tell them where they could be improved.

It is always extremely difficult for a director to handle his peers. I've noticed this in many shows, with stars who have their own particular style which a director would alter at his peril. In our show, the different assumptions led to a paralysing lack of communication which it seemed impossible for anyone to break without giving offence to one party or another.

Bebe was the only one of us to get on with her work, independently of Jack. She was reviving a dance she'd done years before in *Panama Hattie*, and every spare minute found her on stage or in a side room with the adagio team, being tossed from one to the other, going through the most incredible acrobatic feats, to ensure it would be perfect for Blackpool.

Acting she took in her stride, for it was as natural to her as breathing. She had complete faith that the acting and the lines would fall into place eventually. Slowness and delays didn't bother her, so long as she was working on *something*. And as she was well aware she hadn't done much strenuous dancing for years, not a minute was wasted in her pursuit of perfection.

Alas, the rest of us didn't have an adagio dance to keep us occupied, and as the weeks dragged on and we seemed to be making little headway with the play itself, nerves grew taut and tempers very short. As nobody wanted to express doubts to the producer, we lost our tempers with each other, and one morning Ben's rage vented itself on me! He, who was worried to death about his every move on the stage, accused me of 'upstaging' another actress, a small-part player.

I was mortified.

Commonsense should have told me it was a safety valve for him. That he simply had to shout at somebody, for by now he had convinced himself that, in American parlance, we had a 'turkey' on our hands. But I too had become infected with the panicky feeling that Blackpool was going to be a nightmare, and my voice trembled with tears and anger at being so unjustly accused.

I was further incensed over this injustice because I'd worked on the West End stage far more recently than Ben, star or no star, so my awareness of what was or was not up-staging was much more up to date! And I told him so.

I was certainly asking to be thrown out on my ear, if things had been normal! But they weren't. I then stamped down to a position on the stage which satisfied Ben, turned to Jack Hulbert and asked him if this idiotic move was acceptable to him.

The cast froze.

Unpardonably, I had forced our producer to make a decision between me and the star of the show, and he decided in my favour.

Ben threw down his cigar and marched out.

After five minutes he came back.

I waited for the blow to fall. Nothing happened.

Rehearsals were resumed, and suddenly everybody was happy and cheerful. The sudden squall had cleared the air, and we were now at last *working* together instead of brooding together, which made a nice change.

Sandy of course was treated to all the backstage drama when I got home from rehearsals, and marvelled that we could row and argue like this and still remain firm friends and colleagues.

'You're like children,' he said. 'You can get it all out of your systems and forget it ever happened.' He laughed. 'If that were in the City, among ordinary business people, the coolness would last forever.'

But if he despaired of our commonsense, he enjoyed the culinary titbits which were the tasty result of my working in Soho. I was fascinated by the tiny shops of every nationality. I brought home real German sausages, Italian *salami*, Kosher salt beef, French *pâtisserie*, Viennese pastry, not forgetting chocolates from the exclusive establishment which pandered to the sweet tooth of my hero, Churchill. High living indeed. But there was no time for domestic baking sessions, with daily rehearsals in London.

I hadn't tasted Kosher salt beef until Ben took me along one day to a sandwich bar nearby, which had the most delicious hot salt beef sandwiches. I was amazed to discover, though, that because I'd had the beef with my bread, I couldn't have milk with my tea. I had thought Ben was pulling my leg at first, but no, the Jewish faith forbids such foods to be eaten together. I had had no idea that in the midst of all the dubious activities followed in this wicked and colourful area of London, religious and racial taboos were observed so rigidly. And me a Protestant!

Ben laughed when I said that much as I'd enjoyed the salt beef, I'd stick to Lyons' Corner House next time, for I preferred my tea with milk, and non-Kosher establishments didn't give a button what assortment of foods sailed along the alimentary canals of their customers! So long as the bills were paid!

There was little else to lighten the gloom. Rehearsals dragged on, and I began to feel that the luxury of weeks and weeks of rehearsal was something we couldn't afford. It isn't good for people as nervous and mettlesome as actors to work at a dawdling pace. They need an impetus, an acceleration, a sense of excitement, a feeling of pressure that they are working against the clock. Not a weary filling in of weeks as though enthusiasm were gradually winding down. We needed the judgment of an audience. Now!

To add to my personal dismay I now found it would be impossible for me to get home during the entire fifteen weeks. Trains were simply not going to fit our performances. This was a great blow, for I'd looked forward to the cosy sanity of the sweetly familiar domestic background each weekend, imagining I could travel to Pinner after the second house each Saturday and return for the first house on the following Monday. British Railways and the management decreed otherwise, and once the play opened I'd be there for the season.

I'd miss all the summer bulbs, planted with such loving care the previous autumn. I would lose the joy of watching the annuals, grown indoors so painstakingly from seed and transplanted to their final flowering position in spring, attaining their full summer brilliance. I'd miss most of the roses, for they'd be at the end of their flowering by the time I returned in October. October! To be an actress and a gardener is to be torn apart at such times. And it would be almost winter before I could enjoy the comfort of our own bed! A sobering thought.

A look at timetables from the other direction showed us that Sandy could reach Blackpool on Saturdays before I had to leave for the five o'clock performance, but for the return journey on Sunday the only train which would enable him to be at the office on Monday morning meant arriving at Euston at the ungodly hour of four a.m.! This was nearly two hours before the first train left for Pinner, where he could change his clothes, have breakfast, and then go back to town to the office.

It was a punishing routine for him, and ever afterwards when we'd arrive at Euston in the early morning and see tramps and layabouts warming themselves by the radiators and lying in abandoned sleep on benches, he'd remind me, 'That was what I had to do for *fifteen weeks* while you were at Blackpool. Never do that to me again, or I'll leave you to your fate!' I think he meant it!

Not that he need have travelled up every week. It was both tiring and expensive, but he had to reassure himself that I was still surviving the marathon.

My one piece of luck in Blackpool was finding splendid theatrical digs with three spinster sisters within fifteen minutes' sharp walking distance from the theatre. I had selected them from the Equity handbook, with no previous recommendation from anyone, and I landed on my feet. They were to be my salvation during the gruelling Blackpool experience.

I nearly blotted my copybook, though, when I was asked what I would like for my first meal. 'Well,' I said hesitantly, 'I'm too tired to eat a big supper, but I'd love some scrambled eggs. But, eh, how do you make them?' With past experience of watery eggs from tour landladies, I wanted it clearly established right away that I liked mine made with butter or margarine, and with only the smallest permissible amount of milk added, not a sea of liquid to eke out one egg.

Miss Emily, quietly spoken, pale and ladylike, drew herself up and looked at me coldly. 'Olive, my sister, is a beautiful cook,' she said. 'I think you will be pleased with the method she uses. She has worked for the *best* people, and has met with nothing but complete satisfaction.' She turned and left the bed-sitting room before I, obviously *not* one of the best people, could open my mouth either in explanation or apology.

Fifteen minutes later she tapped on the door, and brought in a tray which wouldn't have disgraced the finest hotel in the country. A dish of gently set scrambled eggs under a protective warm cover, a rack of golden toast, a dainty crystal dish of butter balls, home-made jam, a home-made apple pie, biscuits, cheese, and a pot of delicious tea.

Meekly I watched Miss Emily set it out on my table, thanked her, and set to. Every bite went down singing hymns.

The moment I had finished I sought Miss Olive in the kitchen. Plump, dark-eyed, with black hair swept back from a wide forehead, she looked foreign and almost Italian beside her pale slender sister. I seized her hands, determined to make amends at once for daring to question the perfection of her cooking.

'Miss Olive,' I said enthusiastically, 'I've never had anyone serve up scrambled eggs just the way I like them, until now. They were *marvellous*, and I almost licked the plate to get the very last morsel.' A soft but mischievous smile spread slowly over her face, and in a second she, Miss Emily and Miss Nellie were all chattering away nineteen to the dozen, and I knew I was forgiven.

We became real friends, and I write to them still.

When I saw their little courtyard-garden next day I was enchanted to discover they'd used old kitchen sinks as troughs which were filled with wallflower, lobelia and bulbs. Miss Emily was the gardener, and was delighted by my enthusiasm and soon we were away on a discussion of the best fertilizers, the right time to take cuttings, and the sure way to save begonia corms. Every time I look at the three sinks filled with bulbs and plants on the terrace of our house in Pinner I am reminded of the care those three darling ladies took of me, for of course I profited from their example and rescued the old kitchen sink here, the one next door and a third from an old house and turned them into garden troughs.

But to get back to the play. What makes a success in the

theatre, and what whispers the word 'flop' so loudly that you know instinctively that no matter how hard you work nothing is going to make you a hit? If we were able to answer that question with any sort of confidence, there would be no difficulty in getting 'angels' to rush in with cash to back every show which on paper promised well.

We had a week of rehearsals at the Blackpool theatre itself to get the 'feel' of the place before the opening night. And the 'feel' was all wrong. There are theatres where a certain type of show fulfils the expectations of the type of audience which patronizes that particular establishment. Put a brash girlie show in a 'straight' theatre, and your audience will show its disapproval by sitting on its hands at the end and spreading the word around afterwards that the show is a non-starter.

Similarly, put a 'book' show in a variety theatre, and your audience, unused to having to concentrate on a story-line and a continuous plot, will grow restless and uneasy, and reward you with inattention and tepid applause. *And* tell their friends the show wasn't bad, but not all that good either.

In our case we were assuredly in the wrong theatre for a play with music. Vast, musty, comfortless, it normally housed variety, some of it of dubious quality, and the holiday crowd who booked seats in it expected half an hour of *Life with the Lyons* similar to the radio show, with the rest of the bill filled with variety acts. They didn't want to have to follow a plot. They wanted to drift in when it suited them, argue animatedly over where to sit, exchange the odd packet of crisps and bag of sweets, and only when they were comfortably seated and mouths stuffed with snack food would they consider looking up to see what was happening on stage.

All that was to come.

On the opening night we had rehearsed from ten in the morning, which is normal theatrical practice, and curtain up was at six o'clock, for we were performing twice nightly. This was the first time I'd ever heard of a play working to the same schedules as a variety performance, and this factor too may have misled audiences into thinking we were a variety show. There would be exactly half an hour between the first house finishing, and the curtain rising on the second house.

At four o'clock, exhausted with the airlessness of an entire day in this mausoleum of a theatre and a flat feeling of despair that everything was out of phase, I walked over to Jack Hulbert and asked him when we were to have a rest.

He stared at me as if I'd suggested something obscene. Which, in his book, I probably had for he, an actor and producer of sensitivity, was as well aware as any of us how much remained to be done to adapt ourselves to this hangar of a building. 'You don't have a rest,' he said. 'You work till the half-hour before the curtain rises.'

It was my turn to stare at him. I simply couldn't believe my ears. 'What?' I cried. 'Not so much as a breath of reviving fresh air after being in here all day?'

Clearly he felt he was dealing with a lunatic, and turned back to the stage and the piece of business he was checking before I'd so rebelliously interrupted him.

Jack Taylor, the manager of the theatre, was walking about smoking a cigar and shaking his head. It was quite obvious *he* wasn't enjoying this endless dress rehearsal either. Maybe, like our future audiences, he too hadn't realized he was bringing a 'book' show to his rorty-torty theatre. Weel, as the Lord said when the people protested against the flooding rains, he kent noo!

When the curtain rose on our first house performance, the seats weren't even three-quarters filled. Mark you, a few dozen more came in during the first act, and noisily clattered to their seats, making us jump like startled ponies. I was really shaken by this poorly attended house. For the Lyons were beloved throughout Britain, and I was sure they'd pack the theatre. But I hadn't reckoned on the blasé Blackpool holiday-makers, who book for two shows a night throughout their holiday, and are punch-drunk with entertainment and want to be jerked out of their seats with something riveting. Which they didn't find in our show!

With a happy and enthusiastic audience, you don't notice your tiredness. With a tepid reaction and feet moving towards the exits before even one curtain has risen and fallen, failure seeps into the very marrow of your bones and exhausts the will.

We all smiled, of course, and said it was marvellous to be playing to a real live audience at last. But there was no suggestion of a celebration after the second house, and we stared at one another in dismay when Jack Hulbert announced a ten a.m. rehearsal in the morning.

The following ten dispiriting days saw us following exactly the routine of the dress rehearsal.

For Jack Hulbert was a trouper and a trier, and he was determined to do everything in his power to reshape the show to transform us into what our audiences expected.

I'd get home at midnight, lacklustre and jaded from having played to half-empty houses. I grew used to tossing and turning all night, afraid of sleeping in, to have as leisurely a breakfast as possible before the ten a.m. rehearsal call. Working all day in that dusty, musty, airless prison. Half an hour to seize a cup of tea and a sandwich. Curtain up. Two performances. Home to bed, lying staring at the ceiling, wondering what sort of treadmill I was on.

Even the young chorus girls, some barely seventeen years old, were getting a white, pinched look.

Each night the jingle of bells passing the stage door at the end of the first house announced the return of the beach donkeys to their stable, there to find warmth and rest and good food. I envied those allegedly stupid animals from the bottom of my heart. They had had the sense to call it a day. We still had the second house to face.

Since Blackpool I've never seen donkey rides on the sands without remembering the imprisoned feeling of our icy dressing room. For it was bitterly cold weather, more like November than June, and that was no help either in reviving our exhausted spirits. Except of course, that it was better than a heatwave!

One day Jack Hulbert announced that he thought we could break at lunchtime and have the afternoon off. It was the promise of release from Alcatraz! I longed with an intensity which was almost painful for a deep, deep breath of sea air, and two solid hours in bed before I need tread the boards of that stage again. A prisoner promised parole could not have been more ecstatic than I was that morning.

And then, just before one o'clock, the blow fell. Jack Hulbert, perfectionist that he was, turned from the stage where he was altering one of the dance routines, and whispered something to his assistant. 'Back at two o'clock,' she called.

A great wave of shock broke in my throat and I burst into tears. Paradise snatched from me at the eleventh hour was too great a burden to bear. I must have been really at the end of my tether to lose control like this. Everybody had looked shattered at the thought of having to return in the afternoon, but I was hysterical! Me, the even-tempered Scot!

'I can't come back,' I sobbed, making no attempt to hide my despair. I was right over the top now and nothing could stop me. 'You *promised* we wouldn't work this afternoon.'

Even in my own ears I sounded like a child deprived of a treat! A great wail burst from me again: 'I *must* get fresh air, and *sleep*.'

Jack Hulbert froze in mid-step. There was a whispered consultation with his assistant, who came over and patted my shoulder. 'It's all right, Molly,' she said quietly. 'I've told Jack you're not well and he says you can have the afternoon off.'

Diana Dors strolled to the door. When she reached it, she called out to Jack, 'And I'm not coming back either. If the show isn't right by now, another afternoon isn't going to cure it.'

It was terribly unfair to Hulbert, but we were all exhausted. Just as I'm sure he was.

He leaped as if stung. This was defiance which was undermining his authority with a vengeance. Mine was hysteria, Diana's was deliberate mutiny.

'You'll be back here by two o'clock,' he said.

Diana stared at him, a faint smile curling the heavy mouth. 'You can go to hell,' she said, and left the theatre.

It was awful, and I felt it was all my fault for having lost control.

I ran along the seafront, alone, gulping in great breaths of sea air between stifled sobs, and small squeaking prayers to be forgiven for having put such a great man as Hulbert in such an impossible position.

When I reached my digs I crept quietly into the house, sank into bed, and fell into a deep, deep sleep which lasted till Miss Emily tapped on the door with my tea tray. It was like coming up and up and up out of a dark cave. I sat up in bed, dreamy and refreshed after the first decent sleep I'd had since I'd arrived in Blackpool.

When I reached the theatre for the six o'clock performance, the exhaustion of the rest of the cast hit me like a wave of warm foetid air. I felt completely renewed after a mere afternoon's absence from the atmosphere of the place; it was as though I'd been pumped full of vitamins or had just had a blood transfusion. I was dismayed at everyone's tiredness now I could stand back and take a really good look.

I watched the chorus girls, and saw how their leaps had diminished into tiny jumps, a few inches off the floor. They were a bit like zombies, and I knew it was from bone-tiredness.

Doris Rogers told me, with some excitement in spite of her weariness, that Jack Hulbert had been recalled to London for consultations with the London end of the management. News of the afternoon's trauma must have been conveyed to them!

That night when I went to bed, I prayed, on my knees this time, 'Please, God, don't let Jack Hulbert come back to Blackpool. Please, God, don't let him come back. I know he's working to save the show, but we're the ones who have to do it. Please, God, let him stay in London. Please, please, God, and then we can all get some sleep.'

And God answered my prayers.

He was a darling man in himself was Jack, and a hard and dedicated worker, but he was killing us by inches, and God must have decided to put out a helping hand to save us all.

We never saw Jack Hulbert again for the duration of the run. I expect he was glad of this himself, but I couldn't shake off a feeling of guilt that I had started the whole drama of his leaving us. I hope he has forgiven me, if he remembers any of this. Knowing his sunny and gentlemanly character, I expect he held no grudge.

Now we were on our own, and a great gust of activity seized us, as though to prove to Hulbert we really had learned something from all he had taught us in working to save the show.

Richard and I tried interesting and hilarious variations on some of our scenes together, and I marvelled at his ability to change moves and 'business' for the first time before an audience. For we didn't rehearse the changes. We just talked them over together, and then tried them out that same evening. It was stimulating and challenging and we all began to enjoy ourselves.

Bebe was a tower of strength. The audiences, small as they were on most evenings, adored her, and as we did a 'pantomime' curtain-call at the end, with each principal led on by a line of dancers, to take separate applause, I was left in no doubt by the upsurge of clapping on my entrance that they had some liking left over for Aggie too! They seemed to be fond of all the regular members from the radio series. They were simply puzzled by the shape of the show. They missed the variety acts.

I joined the open-air swimming pool, taking out a season ticket, determined to get some health benefit from my stay in Blackpool, and to toughen myself for this twice-nightly stint which I found so heavy.

The attendant was very sympathetic that I had lost many weeks' value because the season had opened at the beginning of June, but I didn't care. If we lasted the full fifteen weeks, I'd still be in pocket, and I knew that having bought the right to go into the pool every day I wouldn't be deterred by cold weather, for I'd want to get my money's worth! It would be a good discipline!

That was the second best thing that happened to me, after my choice of digs, for I now adopted a regime which Sandy called my 'health jag'. I went for a good long walk every morning, and, whatever the weather or the temperature, had half an hour swimming in that enormous salt-water pool. Some days it was so cold that I was the only person in the water. I used to chortle to myself as I puffed across the full width, 'A whole pool to myself. What has a Hollywood film star got that I haven't got?' I'm not a very expert swimmer, but that daily practice so strengthened me that Sandy was quite startled when he came along to watch me one Saturday morning, when he'd managed to travel up the previous day and so was free to come with me for my swim. I was now swimming the length of the bath, along-side the rope it's true, for I wanted a lifeline if I weakened, but it was only there in case of need. I didn't touch it until I'd swum the full length. Sandy declared himself most impressed!

Doris Rogers (Florrie) used to shudder when, in the dressing room we shared, she'd ask, 'You *didn't* go into that pool today, did you?' and I'd reply, 'Yes, of course I did.' 'You must be *quite* mad!' she'd say, staring at me but know-ing I was speaking the truth. She herself felt the cold so much, for the weather was really diabolical with tempera-tures around $50°F$, that for the first time in her life she had taken to wearing a vest! I'd encouraged her in this purchase when she kept shivering, by sensibly pointing out that it was better to be warm and old-fashioned than modern and freezing. Anyway, who was to know she was following my Scots fashion but us? For in spite of my daily dip, I was faithful to my mother's and grannie's prudent teaching and kept the cold at bay with a nice wee semmit.

Doris used to give me my best laugh of the evening by saying, with a sigh, when it came to the moment of truth, 'Now I suppose I'll have to fight my way into my corset.' And fight it was. The Blackpool pork pies and sausages were a constant temptation to which she succumbed only too often, and we both had to do battle with the laces of that corset of hers to make a reasonable streamlining of her curves before she could get into her smart clothes. Dear Doris. I never see those adverts for 'Special Corset Week' in the stores without seeing that nightly struggle to get her laced, and the later relief after the final curtain when we prised her out of her straitjacket!

But if we were now much happier than before, the manager of the theatre, Jack Taylor, was not. The box office reflected the poor business we were doing, and he decided something must be done to attract his former variety audiences.

But what?

Blissfully ignorant of his plans, I was stunned one evening to be told to report to the theatre at two-thirty the following afternoon to rehearse with a new comic, and Bebe. I stared at him in disbelief.

'A new comic?' I stammered. 'How can you write a new comic into a play at this late date? We've been running for three weeks, and we had five weeks' rehearsal in London. The play is "set". We can't alter the plot now, surely!'

But Jack Taylor could.

And did.

With the triumphant air of a conjuror demonstrating a new trick, he produced a wee slapstick comic, Jock, who, it was announced, would be added to the cast of *Life with the Lyons*. How would this stranger be insinuated into the story to make him acceptable to audience and plot alike? Easy! He would be Aggie's boy friend!

I couldn't seriously believe that Bebe would agree to the introduction of this alien character, who had not a word of written dialogue, into a 'book' show. I underestimated her tough flexibility. She was game for anything, and only too willing to listen to any suggestion for improving the appeal of the show. It was only I who was terrified.

The two-thirty rehearsal consisted of Jock, Bebe and me

sitting round a table playing cards. At every mistake I made, Jock, to an imaginary roll of drums, did what he merely described as a 'back-flip' or a 'forward-roll', but as he did not go through the action I had no idea what to expect when we would actually come to do it before an audience. I doubted very much whether we would ever do it. It was probably just to be held in reserve, I assured myself comfortingly. For even as my boy friend the character was, as Tommy Handley would have put it, like a pork chop in a synagogue.

As Aggie I was immaculate in sparkling white apron over gingham dress, with hair swept back into a neat bun, fine black stockings and good black shoes. Jock, splendid and experienced in the world of variety though he was, would have fitted the Glasgow description 'a real wee bauchle'. A flat bunnet topped a small, lined, sallow face. His little compact body was clothed in a tight tweed suit which had seen better days. His breath, to use my mother's graphic assessment, clearly indicated that he 'had looked upon the wine when it was red'. We would never have been attracted to one another in a million years, and the audience would certainly have to suspend belief to accept that we would. I liked him, in spite of my terrors, but we were hardly a matched pair.

At one point in this alleged rehearsal he told me that after a certain line, the only one I *must* say, I was to do a 'cod dry-up'.

'What's that?' I asked him, never having heard the words before.

It was his turn to stare at me. 'Cor blimey,' he said, 'where have you been? A cod dry-up – well, everybody knows what a cod dry-up is.'

'I don't,' I said, flushing at his genuine amazement. 'I've never heard of it.'

93

And I hadn't.

I hadn't worked in the world of variety, apart from my special weeks with Carroll Levis and Henry Hall, and I didn't know of that desperate ruse where the performer pretends he's convulsed with laughter and can't go on with his dialogue, just to get the audience laughing at him, and of course the more they laugh at his apparent discomfiture the more successful the humour seems.

I felt absolutely sick to be asked to indulge in this sort of deception, but Bebe said it wouldn't be seemly for her to do it, and I must. So that was that.

The first rehearsal had been on Thursday afternoon.

The second, which followed the same lines, and left Jock's 'back-flips' and 'forward-rolls' still a mystery, was on the Friday.

On Saturday Jack Taylor decided to spring his brain-child on the second-house audience.

'But how do we get *into* the card sketch?' I asked wildly. 'We have no dialogue.'

'Of course you have,' said Jock, as if I was a half-wit. 'I'll say, "I was standing at the corner of Woolworths, and the *wind* came tearing round the corner" ' – (this was a local holiday joke, apparently) – 'and you say anything you like. We make it up as we go along,' said Jock, encouragingly.

In the middle of a play!

I didn't believe it.

It couldn't be happening. It must be a dream.

Doris Rogers pushed a phosferine tablet into my hand and told me to suck it, for I was shaking so much my teeth were chattering.

The taste was terrible but it seemed to make me feel less sick.

The chorus boys and girls gathered in the wings and all

94

the principals crowded behind them, with stagehands farther back still. They couldn't wait to see what was going to happen.

Behind the inner curtain Jock was flexing his legs like a boxer. There was a roll of drums, and he bounded on to the stage. I heard him say, 'I was standing at the corner of Woolworths, and the *wind* . . .' Where had I heard those words before? Had I dreamed them? Somebody pushed me and I was on.

6

The Saturday audience stirred with interest. Aggie with a strange man. This was something new. Little did they know I hadn't the slightest idea what I was going to do or say.

Jock turned to me. 'Where have you been?' he demanded.

Automatically I replied, in quite a different voice from the rehearsed play, 'I've been looking for you, my lad.' And as the roof didn't fall in at the sound of this deathless prose, I went on, 'My, that's a lovely wee suit you're wearing, when did you buy it?' Jock was clearly delighted with my ad-libbing, and pranced about to show off his tight-fitting shabby jacket and trousers, while the audience rippled with amusement. This was the sort of patter they understood and liked. Shades of Jack Hulbert!

Bebe strolled on, and I flew to her arms like a homing pigeon as Jock turned a back somersault. I could feel her strength and confidence flowing into me as she put her arms round me as though to protect me from Jock's cavortings. Then he suggested a game of cards and we sat down to play. The drum-roll when it came startled me, and I jumped in alarm and nestled into Bebe as Jock threw himself in a magnificent acrobatic double somersault over the back of the chair, retrieved the chair on the return movement and slid it under his bottom, to resume his place at the table.

Uproar!

The audience loved it.

Back to the game of cards again, and the awful moment

when I had to do the 'cod dry-up'. I must have managed it, and it must have meant something to card-players for the place erupted when I said, 'The King of Queens', and Jock leaped into activity again in what he called a 'forward roll'.

The whole thing was completely out of context with the rest of the play. It was unbelievable that a variety act could be used in such a way, involving the star of the show and the maid-cum-housekeeper, but it worked. It was only meant to last about ten minutes, and on that terrible Saturday they were the longest ten minutes of my life. I staggered offstage at the end of this interlude, to much back-slapping and a terrible taste of phosferine in my mouth, glad that I had survived the nightmare.

As the days went on our sketch gradually stretched to a full twenty minutes, and became the highlight of the show. One man used to come in every Saturday for the first house, and he would ask to see me afterwards to see if he had won his bet that this time my laughter had been genuine when I had said, 'The King of Queens.' He would shake his head, baffled, when I'd confess that he was wrong, and that it was a 'cod dry-up'. If I learned nothing else in Blackpool, I learned to deceive the audience with my cod laughter. But I never used it anywhere else. Such tricks didn't really appeal to me. However, it was quite hilarious discovering I could make up dialogue which was acceptable, and I was irresistibly reminded of my childhood when I used to produce the back-court concerts, and hand out the parts on the principle of 'you say that' and 'I'll say this'. It was not exactly Terence Rattigan, nor yet Noël Coward, but our Blackpool audiences didn't mind a scrap, and their unrestrained laughter and applause sweetened the hard work of that season.

Another of Jack Taylor's wheezes almost ended in disaster for me.

Flushed with success over his introduction of Jock to the play, and the delight of the audience in our sketch, he decided he'd enliven the second act with a bit of audience participation in the shape of a competition on the stage. At the end of the first scene in the second act the house lights went on. Members of the audience were invited to volunteer to come up and take part in a horse race, riding on large toy horses which leaped forward jerkily as the mechanism was worked by the feet in the stirrups. The one who reached the footlights first won a prize. They could race six at a time, and it was possible to get through about half a dozen races in about a quarter of an hour. The stagehands had been ordered to get busy and produce prizes, and they made wooden clothes-horses, and mop handles, and similar household goods at minimum cost, which the winners proudly waved aloft to the rest of the audience as they returned to their seats.

The audience were delighted with all this noisy activity, and of course by the end of the races had completely forgotten what the story unfolding on stage was all about. And it was my unhappy task to bring them back, and involve them in the plot. The first time I came on after that first experimental racing competition I was mesmerized by the sight of the winners walking about all over the theatre, showing off their prizes. The house lights were still on to allow them to see where they were going, and nobody was showing the slightest interest in what was happening on the stage. I was all right until Doris Rogers, who was playing Florrie, joined me and said, 'Gorblimey, the audience is on the run!' and rolled her eyes so expressively that I couldn't keep a straight face. It was sheer hysteria, not enjoyment, which made me shake with uncontrollable laughter, and it was a terrible moment for me to feel like this, for the part in the play was approaching when I had to show first Diana

Dors and then Bebe into the room, ready for the confrontation which was to confound and defeat Ben. With my assistance.

I just managed to get through it that night, with seconds to spare before I threw myself into the dressing room, sobbing with hysterical laughter.

But it grew worse with every performance. Doris wickedly knew perfectly well what she was doing to me, for it's all part of the fun and games of a theatre run that the actors try to make one another laugh, or 'dry up' as the stage jargon has it, and she could do all this and not move a muscle herself. But I, shaking and weak with all the weeks of hard work, plus the gastric bug which was affecting most of the company, was quite unable to control the hysteria which rose and threatened to overcome me at that entrance every night.

The fear grew and grew until I couldn't sleep. And then one night, after Doris had made her exit and I had to announce Diana Dors, I just knew I couldn't open my mouth or shrieks of laughter would have burst from me and filled the theatre, and all credibility would have vanished. So I silently beckoned to Diana to come on. She stared at me, outraged. 'Announce me,' she hissed. 'I can't,' I managed to gasp out, in stifled giggles. Bebe was watching from the other side of the wings. Again I beckoned to Miss Dors. Again she hissed, 'You'll bloody well announce me or I won't come on.' This was a nightmare, for Bebe couldn't come on until Diana had been announced or had got on to the stage unannounced.

I could stand it no longer.

I couldn't bear the thought of Bebe's condemnation for my unprofessional behaviour but I could do nothing about it.

I fled.

I reached the dressing room shaking, and began to take

off my clothes, to change into my outfit for my final entrance, sure it was the last time I'd ever do such a thing in that theatre. I was certain I'd be sacked. I'd never be forgiven for racing off the stage, without giving the stars of the show their cues.

Doris had wisely kept silent when she saw how upset I was. There was a knock on the door and the manager came in. Before he could open his mouth, I broke into a torrent of speech. 'I know. I know,' I cried, half-weeping. 'I can't help it. I *can't* go out there night after night, with all the house lights on, and the audience not caring a button what happens, and try to drag them unwillingly into the plot.' And then I added, not pausing to consider I might be 'clyping', as we Scots describe telling tales, 'And Doris Rogers rolls her eyes and makes me laugh.' The manager looked at Doris, murmured something and she left the room.

I think he had thought we were just being unprofessional and undisciplined and playing the fool, until he had entered the dressing room. He didn't know me very well, for I'd never spoken to him beyond the normal 'good evenings' and he had no idea how dedicated I was to my job, and how I'd have cut my tongue out before I would have done anything to jeopardize the play or Bebe's performance.

He told me afterwards that what had convinced him of my sincerity was the fact that I, who normally kept my undies modestly concealed by my dressing gown, was sitting clad only in bra and panties, obviously unaware that I was practically revealing my all! Just like our old neighbour in Springburn, I realized with a spasm of surprise, who'd run down to rescue her little daughter who'd been caught in the cow-catcher of a tram, unaware that she was standing right out in the street dressed only in her camisole and skirt.* I must have been in a similar state of shock.

*Shoes were for Sunday, Hutchinson, 1970.

Seeing my agitation and understanding its cause, his manner changed completely. He was very sympathetic and very wise. He gave me some practical advice as to how I could cope with this situation. I was to say to myself before I went on, 'This is *Hamlet* I am playing in. It is a very tragic play and I must give it my full sober concentration, whatever is happening out there in the audience.' He also advised me to change my position at the table when Doris joined me, so that I need not meet her eyes.

He, for his part, would see to it that the house lights went out before the play resumed, because it was ridiculous that actors be asked to perform with the whole theatre illuminated. Darkness focused audience attention on the stage, and darkness we would have.

Next night I followed his advice, although Doris was livid that I had changed my position at the table without a word to her. I confessed that I had deliberately kept silent, because I suspected she would simply have adjusted her own move and we'd have been eyeball to eyeball again. I did something else to break this hypnotic stare of poor Doris which had reduced me to hysterics. I had been reading James Joyce, and each night at the end of my *Hamlet* incantation, I added as a safeguard, 'And I'm not going to bother about her. She's just a big fat tottie!'

It was awful of me, but I was desperate.

It worked!

I think the manager must have explained everything to Bebe, for she accepted my apologies quietly and graciously. Diana Dors had obviously also been informed, for she too just grinned and said, 'Forget it.'

I don't think anything bothered Diana for long. She could even take a lawsuit in her stride, and appeared in the courts near Blackpool in the afternoon before doing two shows with us at night. Whatever the offence was (I think it was a tax mix-up), it had happened before her twenty-first birthday and because it involved money her earnings had to be revealed.

The judge had said, with heavy sarcasm, 'Who is this minor, who is unable to manage her affairs, but whose earnings are above those of top management?'

Everybody seemed to know the case was being tried, for the streets were packed with fans when it was over. As she emerged and stood at the top of the steps, somebody in the crowd shouted out, 'What was the verdict, Diana?' Without a pause she grinned and called back, 'Guilty, but insane!'

She had a very lively sense of humour, and also an unexpected sensitivity at times. One afternoon she'd been invited to go round a shoe factory and that night as we stood in the wings she murmured to me, 'God, fancy having to stand at a bench, and make those slippers eight hours a day. Then I really *would* go mad.' I was quite taken aback at such a reaction from the cool Diana.

She simply couldn't understand my nervous tension before every performance. 'What are you worrying about?' she'd demand, as we waited together for an entrance. 'Those gobs out there couldn't do it!' Maybe they couldn't, but that was no comfort to me waiting to tackle yet again this peculiar show with its variety card-act and race-competition grafted on to it, mostly to my discomfiture.

But Bebe was a tower of strength, and an example to all of us if we felt like flagging. During that strenuous adagio dance she strained a ligament one night when she landed awkwardly, but didn't miss a beat. She had the leg strapped up so that it didn't show under her tights, although a heavier support would have been more help, and she went through that taxing routine twice nightly, with never a word of complaint.

Later in the run she had to have an impacted wisdom tooth extracted in the afternoon. She went on that night just the same – two performances as usual – and never cut a single number. I only knew about it because as we stood in the wings she had a box of tissues placed in readiness so that she could deal with any bleeding, between her entrances.

I used to tell her she'd go on if she were dying. 'Sure I would, honey,' she agreed happily. 'And sometimes I'm darn near it!' I believed her.

Barbara celebrated her twenty-first birthday in Blackpool, and that was the only party I attended. I always hared straight back to the digs and bed after the show, but a twenty-first birthday was a different matter. It was held in a lovely hotel in St Anne's, where the family had their rented house, and the most memorable part of it was that Barbara gave me a lovely big box of chocolates somebody had given to her, for she didn't want to be tempted to eat them and ruin her diet. Weight was an ever-pressing problem for her, and I was delighted to remove temptation from her path!

That box of chocolates was as good as a tonic to me. My appetite was very poor, for I couldn't seem to shake off the effects of the gastric bug. I wasn't alone in this, mark you, for the whole of Blackpool was affected and actors were going down like ninepins at every theatre. However, I sampled a chocolate that night with my bedtime cup of tea, and it was like rediscovering a forgotten delight. Chocolates had gone completely out of my life during the traumas of this play, and it was a joy to find myself actually tasting and smacking my lips over anything I was eating.

They brought my appetite back as though they'd been filled with quinine or iron, and my very enthusiasm for them was a welcome sign that I was feeling better.

And then, suddenly, it was all over. Crowds were thinning, the theatres were feeling the pinch, and we'd all had enough. It was like a reprieve. A whole week before we'd expected it. I rang Sandy to announce the glad tidings, and told him not to bother coming up that Saturday, for I'd be home next day, with the rest of the company. 'I'd better give the house a good clean then,' he chortled. 'That's a better deal than lying on the station radiators waiting for the first morning train to Pinner.'

Diana Dors declared she was going straight into a convent, to rest after the sight of all those milling crowds, racing to and from the station with their suitcases on barrows each Saturday as the holiday traffic changed over!

Ben quietly went into the London Clinic to recover from a pulled muscle he'd sustained during a hectic dance in the finale one night, and Richard followed him to have his appendix out!

I visited them both, and they nearly had a relapse laughing over all the Blackpool adventures, which already seemed in the past, and wildly funny now that they were all over.

If poetry is emotion recollected in tranquillity, comedy is surely nightmares recollected when there's little chance of their being repeated!

It was sheer heaven for me to be home, even if there were only a few roses on the bushes to remind me that I had missed the summer's glory in the garden. To be free to do what I pleased. To bake, to cook, to clean, to write, to have visitors or not as I chose, and to sit and read or listen to the radio with never a thought of a demanding curtain about to go up.

And Sandy was like the cat who's swallowed the cream, to find a nice meal and a light in the window when he returned from the office, and as much of my chatter as he could stand! 'Glad to have you aboard, ma'am,' he'd reply, when I asked if it was nice to have the cook back in the kitchen.

I hadn't heard anything of my friend Joan Harben while I was in Blackpool, and before I had time to ring her to tell her all about the stage adventures which I knew would be greeted with appalled giggles, for she was a creature of the legitimate theatre and would understand every last nuance, I had a phone call from another actress friend.

'Have you heard about Joan Harben?' she asked me.

My heart gave a lurch.

'No,' I stammered. 'Has something happened?'

'I hear she is dying,' said my friend. 'I hear she has cancer.'

I was stricken. I couldn't believe it. And yet when I remembered the pale fine-drawn appearance last time we'd met, and the death-like pallor when she'd collapsed during an *ITMA* rehearsal, a tight knot of apprehension twisted and grew until I found I was shaking.

I stared at the telephone. Should I ring her house? What would I do if Clive answered and told me the worst?

I dialled her number, my hand clenching the receiver. Joan's voice answered. 'Oh hu-llo, Molly,' she called out, voice vibrant and strong as ever. I was so relieved I almost burst into tears. Then a great wave of anger flooded over me, at the thought of that actress telling me such a wicked rumour, when Joan was her normal, friendly, strong-sounding self.

When I'd told her sketchily about the finish of the Blackpool season, I said, trying to put it as mildly as possible, 'And how are you, Joan? I heard you weren't very well.'

There was a brief pause. 'I'm not,' she said quietly. 'And it's the worst.'

My heart turned over. 'Oh, my God,' I thought, 'it's true. It wasn't a rumour. She *is* dying.' If Joan Harben admitted it was the worst, then it was.

Before I could find my voice she went on, 'But I'm not going to give up hope. I have so much to live for. Clive and I have a wonderful life, and Penny is at the most exciting and interesting stage. I am simply going to live. I am not giving up.'

I laughed shakily. 'That's the spirit, Joan,' I said. 'Just you have faith that you'll get better, for we all know that faith can move mountains.'

We talked for a little longer, but decided we wouldn't arrange a meeting just yet, for she wasn't coming into town at the moment and was resting a lot.

A few days later I opened my paper and on the front page was a photograph of Joan, and underneath the words, 'Mona Lott dies at 47.'

And I remembered her looking round all our faces during an *ITMA* rehearsal one day and saying to me, wonderingly, 'Do you know, Molly, I think I'm almost the oldest person here.'

And yet she was only forty-seven when she died, and that didn't seem old at all.

And she was so beloved in her character of Mona Lott, whose catchphrase 'It's being so cheerful as keeps me going' was echoed by the nation, that her death had gained that coveted publicity prize, the front page of the national press.

I wept for the loss of a dear friend and colleague, and for the silent emptiness to be faced by Clive and Penny. I learned afterwards that with her dying breath, she had taken the hands of the minister at the bedside and had gazed into his face with complete trust and said, 'I'm not going to die. I have faith. I am going to be all right.' She had then turned and smiled radiantly to Clive standing at the other side of the bed, closed her eyes and fallen asleep, never to waken this side of the grave.

The minister himself had been moved to tears, and said he had never in all the years of his ministry seen such gentle trust and complete unquestioning faith.

She was a lovely person, and even in the year that I write these words, her catchphrase is quoted by the newspapers as a headline over the latest food price rises, tax increases and other domestic disasters. It moves my heart to remember that she lived and died by that philosophy.

She and I had both been catapulted into the headlines because of our involvement with *ITMA*, and we could never get over the interest the press and public had in us. I found I was now in great demand to open bazaars, open radio shows, launch charity appeals, and lend my name and presence anywhere when the organizers wanted a figurehead who would draw the crowds.

At first I used to rehearse my opening speech as though it were a stage performance, until I grew so used to these affairs that I just asked for details in the car *en route* to the opening, and incorporated them in my remarks from the dais. I had to have quite a wardrobe of 'public appearance' clothes, for when people turn up to meet a well-known personality, they want an eyefull of interesting clothes as well! Sales found me acquiring all sorts of dressy items I'd never have dreamed of wearing in my ordinary everyday life. End-of-range models from Jacqmar, in fine navy wool crêpe-de-chine, coat-dresses in soft tartans, stunning hats, even a fur stole from Barbara Lyon's furrier, who made one for me of smaller proportions to suit my tiny build. I was charmed with this last item, until a candid friend told me I looked like a *nouveau-riche* social climber, carrying her cash round her shoulders! That, I may say, was the stole's final appearance on any platform! Such a pity, for it was a beauty and I'd saved for a whole year to buy it.

One lovely summer fête which I was asked to open was a splendid affair. It was in the grounds of a beautiful house in the country, to which I was whisked in a very grand chauffeur-driven car. After the opening, where my opening remarks were greeted with warm laughter and applause, I found myself sitting at tea opposite a very handsome, distinguished gentleman, with silvery hair and attractive voice, and there was something familiar in his appearance which intrigued me. I was certain I'd never met him before. I was also certain he wasn't an actor, whose face might have impressed itself on my memory through stage appearances, and yet there was a teasing likeness which puzzled me.

And then my ears sorted out the jumble of names which had been murmured during the introductions of several people, and I caught my breath with excitement. 'Bowes-Lyon. Bowes-Lyon. David Bowes-Lyon.' He was the favourite brother of the Queen Mother, who at that time, of course, was our Queen, and it was the family resemblance which I had spotted.

My word. What would my mother say when I told her I was sitting passing the cakes to the Queen's brother! Oh gosh, and I'd promised to bake him a home-made loaf and send it to him, when, not knowing who he was, we'd been discussing the domestic arts and he'd declared that one of the things he missed most in life was home-baked bread.

I would have kept my promise about the bread, but Sandy was aghast at the very idea of sending a wrapped loaf of mine to near-royalty, so I undid the foil-covered bread and put it beside our own in the bread-tin. But when, very soon afterwards, I read that he had died, I grieved over my broken promise, and hoped this beloved brother of the Queen hadn't dismissed me as a flibbertygibbet of an actress who'd betrayed the integrity of the true Scot whose word is his bond.

As well as being asked to do appearances on my own I was also now being asked to appear as one of the 'family' with the Lyons, and we attended fan club dinners and dances, visited factories, and judged competitions. Having sold my unloved squirrel coat, I had no fur coat, and I was forever drooling over Barbara's and Bebe's mink coats. I discovered one very satisfying fact about mink. Unlike most luxury items, it is strong and hard-wearing. Like diamonds, it hardly ever wears out. It may go out of fashion, or it may slightly lighten with the years, but it remains warm, glossy, and beautiful. I noticed how, whatever they had on underneath, Bebe and Barbara always looked like a million dollars in their minks. I also noticed it needed no special cosseting, this covetable fur. It could be thrown down, used as a knee-wrap, bundled into the car, and it took no harm. I determined to save up for one. Especially after Ben, seeing me draping myself yet again in Bebe's, had said, 'Why don't you invest in one, honey? With all the public appearances you do, you need never think of another winter coat, and you needn't buy a new mink. You can go to an auction, and get a good one second-hand, but take somebody with you who knows something about furs.'

That was enough to set me off in hot pursuit of my dream. A mink coat! Sandy agreed it would be a good idea, now that I was making so many personal appearances, and often coming home very late in extremely cold weather.

When I'd saved up what I thought was sufficient, I rang up Anne Crawford, that beautiful actress from Edinburgh who was a big name in British films. We'd met in a show and been good friends thereafter. 'How about coming with me to a fur auction, Anne?' I asked. She'd love to, she told me, but she had an appointment at University College

Hospital for a blood test. It appeared she had to go regularly, for some sort of glandular disorder. Nothing vital about it, and she could switch dates easily. When I told her that one week was as good as the next for me, for they held such auctions regularly, she laughed and said she'd far rather go to a fur auction with me than go to the hospital for a routine check. So she cancelled her appointment and we headed for town.

It was absolutely enthralling. I'd never *seen* such beautiful furs. I couldn't believe they were second-hand, or that anybody could bear to part with such beauties. But Anne was far more knowledgeable. 'Old-fashioned shoulders,' she'd hiss, 'and it costs a fortune for mink alterations.' Or, 'Too light – faded – it's seen at least ten years' wear.' Or, 'Too heavy for you, Molly. You want a slimmer line.'

She was a tower of strength.

After a half-dozen auctions, I was beginning to get my eye in, and I also had a better idea of prices.

One day Bob Beattie's wife asked Anne if she could join us and we went along to a salon off Bond Street, I quite determined that this time I'd buy something, Mrs Beattie just coming along for the ride as it were.

We hadn't been looking five minutes when Mrs B. was riveted by the sight of a gorgeous dark brown silky mink, full length, which was just her size. She tried it on. Perfect. She was in a fever of excitement. 'But you didn't mean to buy a mink,' I said, trying to steer her away from a purchase she could regret next day, for surely such an expensive item shouldn't be bought on impulse!

Swiftly she calculated that the money they'd saved to install central heating would be just enough to buy the coat. She was deaf to reason. The model paraded the catwalk half an hour later. Mrs B. was in there with the bidding from the word go, and a cheque for the exact amount which had been earmarked for central heating was exchanged for a mink coat.

I got nothing.

When Bob came to collect her his amused reaction to her purchase staggered me. Instead of flying into a rage, as could have been expected, he shrugged his shoulders, cocked an eyebrow in amusement and said, 'How do you like that? She's the only one who will be warm in her mink, and the rest of us in the house can freeze to death!'

I thought it was a marvellous attitude to take, especially when it was his money, and it was yet another example that an adored wife could get away with murder!

The fur auctions were drawing to a close, for it was coming on for summer, and Anne Crawford had to go into hospital anyway for some further checking, and I decided my mink plans were going to have to be shelved for another season.

And then an actress friend took me along to her furrier to put her furs in store during the hot weather (a very luxurious touch, this, I thought), and she laughingly asked him if he couldn't find a little mink coat for me somewhere among his rich clients. I wouldn't have had the nerve to suggest this myself, for I thought furriers wanted only to sell new coats, where the biggest profit would be made. 'How much do you want to spend?' he asked me. I told him. He pursed his lips. 'Leave it to me,' he said, 'and I'll see what I can do.'

This wasn't as much fun as the auctions, but it wasn't so chancy either. He was a furrier with a high reputation, and his honesty was guaranteed by my actress friend.

I went up to Glasgow in the summer to collect my mother and bring her back to Pinner to spend a month with us. One morning, as she sat reading her newspaper, sipping the tea I'd handed in to her in bed, she said, 'Oh my, isn't this awfu' vexin' aboot poor Annie Crawford?' She called her 'Annie' with the Glasgow familiarity, not recognizing Anne as a name at all. 'What's vexing about Anne?' I said, seizing the paper.

Anne's serenely beautiful face stared at me from the centre page. 'Anne Crawford dies at 35 from leukaemia.'

Tears slid down my cheeks as I read that she had been attending University College Hospital for some time, as it was known from tests that she had contracted this incurable disease. She herself had had no suspicion. Nor had I.

'Oh, Anne, Anne,' I cried to myself. 'Fancy me trailing you round fur auctions, and you cancelling hospital appointments!' And yet one small corner of my mind remembered our laughter and the fun we had had, planning our campaign and our strategy over restorative cups of tea and delicious *pâtisserie*. It was surely a happier fate for such a lovely young woman to live normally and enthusiastically every moment which was hers than to sit morbidly waiting for the end. But it was cruelly young to be taken.

I never look at my mink without remembering Anne Crawford and the auction rooms.

For I did get the coat before the end of that summer.

My friend's furrier was making a dyed ermine coat for one of the royal duchesses who was about my size. He had asked her if she would sell him her mink, as he had a little client very eager to acquire one, and who couldn't afford a new one.

'Why should I sell it?' she'd asked. 'I like it.'

'But you don't need it,' he'd pressed gently. 'You'll have five full-length fur coats when I've finished this ermine.' Then he added, 'And she's a hard-working little actress, who's saved every penny of it herself.'

'Oh, all right,' she'd said at last. 'But I want a good price for it, for I don't really want to sell it at all.'

He paid her exactly what I said I could afford, and the coat didn't require a single alteration.

It was (and is!) a soft, chocolate brown, thick-pelted mink, mid-calf length, and a beautiful protection against the worst that the weather can do. It has been soaked with rain, it has served as a blanket in cold trains, to my mother's horror, and it has come up smiling.

My mother, whose ideas of prices went no further than a hundred pounds, made me shake with suppressed laughter, when she stopped one day to admire a musquash coat in a fur sale. It was priced at eighty-five pounds. 'Look at that,' she said. 'It's no' a patch on your ain fur coat, and it's near enough a hunner pounds.'

'I should think not indeed,' I murmured.

My mother never knew it was mink I was wearing.

I wouldn't have dared tell her.

She'd have thought I was going 'straight to the dogs', wearing what she'd have described as 'a king's ransom' on my back.

7

The first interesting job I was asked to do after the acquisition of the mink coat was to judge a cheese-eating competition at Glasgow Kelvin Hall food exhibition with Sir Compton Mackenzie. I'd never met him before, and I was agog to see the brilliant writer in person at long last. I'd read most of his books, and had been enslaved by *The Four Winds of Love* to the point of tears.

Margaret Patten and I were also to judge a cookery contest organized for the schoolchildren, who were to grill herrings and bake oven scones. We were staying at the Central Hotel, which thrilled my mother to the core. She'd never been inside its famous portals, and couldn't believe such grandeur had been laid on for me just because I was acting as a judge in a mere cheese competition. But she adored having tea and sandwiches served to us in my room, and was most impressed by the waiter in his tailcoat, who flourished the napkins and whisked the silver plate with the expertise of a conjuror.

'By jings, they'll chairge ye something for a' this!' she said, pursing her lips, but unable to hide the sparkle in her eyes at the thought of describing this glimpse of high living to her favourite neighbour.

If she thought the room service might be expensive, I don't know what she'd have thought of the hairdressing salon Margaret and I had to visit to repair the ravages of

Glasgow's wind and weather. We'd had our hair soaked when we'd gone out to fulfil a lunch engagement, and decided we must have it properly shampooed and set for our evening appearance at Kelvin Hall.

Half a dozen assistants fluttered round us, and the whole performance took about twice as long as we were used to in our own hairdresser's in London. We were both in the habit of paying around eighteen shillings for a shampoo and set, an average price at a first-class hairdresser's at that time, so you can imagine we were rocked on our heels to be presented with bills of £4 15s and £5 (Margaret had been talked into having a friction and that accounted for the odd five shillings).

To add insult to injury the head assistant had the audacity to whisk open a drawer as I searched my purse for the necessary cash, and produce a glittering butterfly which he placed against my hair. He closed his eyes with exaggerated ecstasy and said, 'Now, this ornament would just finish you off, madam. Only thirty-five shillings.'

I looked him straight in the eye. 'A hair-do at £4 15s needs no other ornament than the bill,' I said. 'If I pin anything at all to this expensive edifice, it will be *that* – receipted!'

Margaret giggled at my nerve, but declared she was keeping her bill to show it to her income-tax accountant.

I didn't meet Sir Compton until we took our places on the platform to judge the cheese-eating competition. It was the first time I'd seen an eating competition of any description, and I was appalled. All the contestants had huge chunks of cheese on a table in front of them (no ladies entered, I was interested to note!) and when the bell sounded they tore lumps off and crammed them into their mouths until their eyes were bulging. Jaws champed furiously, pieces of cheese fell to the ground, crumbs fell inside shirts, one man choked and brought up everything he'd eaten!

Sir Compton gazed fastidiously on this orgy, and seemed as glad as I was when the bell sounded and the winner was proclaimed.

A cheese shaped like a haggis was piped on to the platform and placed on the table in front of us. The organizers had a tiny little glass of whisky in readiness for the piper, in accordance with the tradition at Burns Suppers. Sir Compton gazed on the thimbleful of whisky with disdain. 'Good God, man,' he said to the English organizer, 'you can't offer a piper a dram of that size. Give him a real drink.'

Shaken by this criticism, the man went to the other extreme, and poured out a full tumbler, to the brim. Traditionally, the piper has to raise the glass to his lips and drain it in one swallow. I watched, fascinated, as the piper raised this full tumbler to his lips. He hesitated for a fraction of a second, then nobly downed the lot. Perspiration burst from his forehead as a full quarter-pint of whisky hit his stomach, then, with glazed eyes he turned to face the audience, and with the merest hint of a stagger made his way down the full length of the hall. I raised my hat to him, and hoped he didn't fall flat on his face the minute the air reached him!

Sir Compton was taken on a tour of the exhibition while Margaret and I judged the children's efforts. The smell of grilling herrings filled the nostrils, and it was delightful to see the serious concentration of the boys and girls as they prepared to serve their food on the platters, ready for our inspection. One wee lad, flushed with nervous excitement, lifted the grill pan carefully, to lay it alongside the serving plate. It tilted disastrously, and the herrings catapulted and landed smack on the floor at his feet. He raised a piteous face, eyes brimming with tears, lips trembling.

I slipped quietly over to him. 'Wait a minute, son,' I said in a whisper. 'We'll just lift them up with the fish-slice and slip them on to the plate. They're beautifully cooked and that's what matters, and we have to cut them anyway to make sure they're cooked right through.' As we lifted them to the plate, I added, 'You can always give them to the cat, if you don't want to eat them off the floor.'

'We hivnae goat a cat,' he said, 'but ma auntie has, and I'll gi'e them to her.'

His scones were perfection, and he won a 'place' for the quality of his cooking. When he came to receive his certificate, I winked at him, and he pressed his lips together to stop himself from giggling. I wonder if he went on to become a chef? And I wonder if he was glad he never ate in our house, because I was quite capable of scraping food off the floor and making a decent show of it!

After all this was over, we were taken back to the hotel to dine in the Malmaison. A little three-piece orchestra was playing in a small gallery above the restaurant. At sight of Mackenzie they immediately broke into the strains of the signature tune from his marvellous film *Whisky Galore*, and the whole restaurant stood up and applauded him. I've seldom been so moved or so thrilled at such public acknowledgement of a great figure in such a spontaneous gesture.

It was a tremendous moment.

When we reached the table somebody draped my mink coat over the back of my chair. I looked at the menu and saw we were to start with soup, and then go on to other dishes which had gravy, and finally to sweets with cream. I've never trusted the deft hands of waiters since I saw a whole plate of soup tipped over a lady's coat in a hotel dining room, and I began to fear for my precious mink. Seeing my restlessness, Sir Compton suggested I have it put in the cloakroom. 'No, I don't want to do that,' I said in a whisper. 'It's brand-new and I'm frightened to let it out of my sight.' I was sure that to see such a fine coat was to covet it!

With a shout of laughter Sir Compton took it from me, demanded that a coat-stand be brought and placed opposite our table where it was in sight while we ate, and announced to all the waiters, 'Now for God's sake don't spill a drop of food anywhere near that coat. It's Molly's. It's brand-new. And she won't eat a bite unless she can keep it in view every second of her life.'

It was hilarious, and in spite of my blushes I had to admit it was a great idea. All during the meal he kept checking, 'Coat still all right? *That's* good!'

The waiters entered into the spirit of the fun, and watched with exaggerated care as they passed the coat-stand with their plates and platters. I think the restaurant thought we were quite mad.

I found Mackenzie a stimulating dinner companion. He kept the whole table enthralled with his tales of Greece, and of people in high places. We spoke of his books, and it seemed incredible to me that here I was sitting in the Malmaison in Glasgow actually discussing with their author those enchanting characters in *The Four Winds of Love*. He was very handsome, and assuredly one of the most attractive personalities I've ever met. We had to race along the platform to catch our night sleeper. I never saw him again.

I'd managed to make this Glasgow visit between our recordings for *Life with the Lyons* for we were back again with our radio series. What bliss just to have to do one show per week in front of a mike and our faithful audience instead of twice nightly to indifferent Blackpool holiday-makers.

Gwen Lewis, who played Mrs Wimple, had written a rare wee song for me called 'Aggie who feeds the Lyons' and I recorded it for a gramophone company, with 'Glasgow' on the other side. It didn't actually set the Clyde on fire, although a New Zealand station used the first side as a signature tune for one of their programmes. Alas, they had a reciprocal arrangement with Britain, and I never got a penny piece for their daily use of my record. 'Twas ever thus!

I think I made about ten shillings altogether from that record – a clear sign that I had no future as a pop star!

But Gwen's song was a lifesaver when it came to opening future bazaars and fêtes. I had the bright notion of using the first verse instead of a speech as such, for the Lyons were at the height of their popularity, and anything which incorporated this zany, lovable family was sure to amuse. Also it made a different opening, quite unique to me and to our show, and I used it for years. It went:

> No doubt you have seen Philip Harben
> Many times on the TV screen.
> He looks rather weird, with that funny wee beard,
> The one who makes omelettes, I mean.
> Well, if you know him, you can't fail to know me –
> We're the two best-known cooks on the BBC.
>
> I'm Aggie who feeds the Lyons,
> And I don't mean the ones in the zoo.
> Though the name is the same,
> Their radio fame is very well known to you.
> They're a nice little family party,
> And they think that my cooking's a boon.
> I've been with them for years,
> And they're ever such dears,
> To Aggie from Glasgow Toon.

Gwen was delighted to know I was making regular use of her lyrics in this way, and she also wrote several numbers which I used in *Workers' Playtime*, which I was asked to do by Bill Gates. We visited factories and entertained them in their lunch-hour, in the canteens, where the shows were broadcast live. I devised a sketch as the ice-cream girl in the cinema, and Gwen wrote a lyric which started, 'I'm Aggie the girl with the ices, I'm Aggie the girl with the tray.'

Another sketch I wrote was all about my boy friend Dodie, and Gwen wrote a number incorporating his pinch-penny character as described by me, which started, 'Ma Dodie isn't generous, tho' he's not exactly mean, But I wouldn't say that to anyone else but you.'

I did this Dodie sketch and song for Henry Hall in one of his Guest Nights from the Paris Cinema, to celebrate St Andrew's Night when Ruby Murray was on the bill. She was a very big name at that time, and was top of the bill at the Palladium that week. She was most impressed by my being able to get up and tell jokes, for she was terribly nervous, and her speaking voice was so choked with husky terror I didn't know how she'd ever get a note out when she sang. She did, of course, and sang truly and sweetly.

'But, Ruby,' I said to her, 'if you're as nervous as this for a small audience in a radio studio, how on earth do you manage to go out on stage at the Palladium every night?'

She gave a soft sad smile.

'I'm feart every night,' she confessed.

Her mother gave me a great laugh when she sat watching four male singers going through their routine at rehearsal. They were pretty mature, and they went through a gentle bit of tap-dancing during the opening bars of the music, and between the numbers. Shaking her head with disapproval, she said, 'Them men's faur too old to be kickin' up their legs like that.'

'Don't let them hear you say that,' I gasped, shaking with laughter. She might have been my own mother talking.

Jean Campbell was also on the bill, a very popular Scots singer, and because it was St Andrew's Night she sang 'My Ain Folk'. Now I've hardly ever been able to get through that touching, heart-stirring song of home-sickness without tears, and as she was on just ahead of me, I hoped I wouldn't make a fool of myself and find myself gulping with sobs when I ought to have been cracking jokes! To my amazement Jean came off with the tears running down her cheeks, 'Oh *why* did I sing that?' she wept. 'I might have *known* I'd never get through it, especially on St Andrew's Night.' So it wasn't just me who was so sentimental that a song could pierce the heart.

We sucked butterscotch afterwards, to calm ourselves down for the final bows and farewells, another taste we shared. All Scots seem to have a very sweet tooth. I know the Lyons were highly amused at first when I was always able to produce a sweetie during rehearsals. In fact they got to the stage when, if they grew hungry, they'd come over and say, 'Give us one of your sweets, Aggie.'

Eventually, Ben used to send one of the boys out on Wednesdays when we met at the Paris to do our recording, to buy a large assortment of toffees and boilings for the cast and orchestra. He used to throw sweeties to Paul Fenhoulet and the boys up on the stage during rehearsal, and they'd catch the brightly wrapped sweets as though fielding cricket balls. He'd also distribute them to us at various times during the run-through. This led to his playing a ghastly joke on me one day.

At this particular rehearsal Ben came up to me and handed me a long sweet wrapped in silver paper. 'Like a sweet, Aggie?' he asked me casually. 'Oh yes, thanks, Ben,'

I said, thinking he was being very polite in handing it to me instead of shouting 'Catch' as he usually did. I took the silver paper off, put the sweetie in my mouth and started chewing.

It tasted a bit waxy, and as I chewed, wondering what sort of flavour this was, Ben was doubled up in laughter, wheezing and clutching his sides. When he could speak, he gasped, 'Spit it out, Aggie, spit it out. It's a suppository!'

I'd never seen one before, so had suspected nothing.

'Ben Lyon,' I yelled, affronted, 'you're a big brute!'

Ben, of course, couldn't believe I hadn't known what it was, and had merely expected me to be shocked at his offering it to me, for he was always pulling my leg. And he'd been so staggered at my actually thinking it *was* a sweet, he'd let me put it in my mouth and try to eat it.

He delighted in reminding me of this incident for years, and whenever a new guest appeared on our show he told the story all over again, finishing up with, 'She'd eat anything, of course, if it was a sweetie and it was for nothing!'

And then he'd go into roars of laughter all over again. It was almost worth the rotten taste for the fun we got from that caper down through the years, and it didn't do me a bit of harm after all.

It was Ben who inspired the purchase of our first TV set. He'd say to me when we met for rehearsal, 'Did you see that show on TV last night?' to which I automatically responded, 'We haven't got a TV set, Ben. I don't really want one. I've far too much to do, learning, reading, working, I haven't time to sit watching TV.'

TV was just getting into its stride in this country, after all the post-war shortages, but only a comparatively few people had sets. Radio was still the main entertainment, and anyone in a radio series was a household name.

Ben always countered my obstinacy in considering buying a set with, 'You ought to have one, honey. In our business we have to know what's going on.'

Sandy was curious about the new medium, but I really hadn't the slightest interest in sitting in front of a screen at home, wasting time.

Then the excitement started building up for the Coronation of Queen Elizabeth II in the summer of 1953, and British Actors' Equity had a block of seats in a section of the seating in Piccadilly. A ballot would be held, and seats were £4 each. 'You haven't an earthly,' Sandy had said when I told him I was going to ballot for seats. 'Everybody will think that,' I said, for there were thousands of actors and only about two hundred seats, 'So the ones with faith, like me, will have every chance in the world.'

I was right. We were allotted two seats, although Sandy thought we were mad to spend £8 to sit in the street for hours, for we had to be in our places by half past seven in the morning. And it might well rain all day!

Then it dawned on me that the Coronation would take place while my mother was down with us on her annual holiday. 'We can't leave her at home all day alone,' said ever-thoughtful Sandy, who saw his chance to acquire a TV at long last. 'We know we'll have to get TV some time, so we might just as well get it now, and she can watch the whole ceremony at home.'

'*Very* thoughtful,' I said, 'and *very* clever!'

So we bought a fourteen-inch Pye and it was duly installed in the cold sitting room, which we only used when we had visitors. Old habits die hard, and we kept to the Glasgow custom of a 'best' room for entertaining, while we used the warm living room at other times when we were alone. We had open coal fires, but coal was still in short supply and we couldn't get enough to keep two open fires going. We lit the sitting room fire only when people were visiting us.

I deliberately had the TV put in the sitting room, so that it would just be used occasionally. I was still determined not to be a slave to sitting there, immobilized, in front of it.

As we read, or listened in, or chatted, Sandy would say to me, 'Are you not curious about what's going on next door on that TV screen?' 'No,' I'd answer truthfully, for I didn't even look up the *Radio Times* to see what was on.

He would steal through occasionally, and I'd find him standing looking at the blank screen. 'Fancy, all sorts of things going on there,' he'd say, 'and us sitting next door not even bothering.'

Then one very cold night he decided it was time the sitting room had a fire to keep all the furniture properly aired, and we watched our first TV for a whole evening.

We never went back to the living room.

We were hooked.

My mother was entranced to have 'the pictures' in the house, as were my cousin and her new husband who were on honeymoon from Australia, and who had found a bed with my kindly next-door neighbour so that they could be near us. We hadn't room for them when my mother was with us, but they were eager to be within easy reach of us – and our television!

When the alarm went off at five-thirty a.m. on the morning of the Coronation there was a strange feeling of disbelief that the great day had actually arrived. We had all talked and read about it for so many months that the actual moment had a dreamlike quality. We ate our breakfast in a calm yet excited silence, checked over the contents of the picnic basket, cut some roses for our buttonholes and went out into the biting cold of a day which might have been February instead of June.

To my mother's horror, for nobody in their senses in Glasgow would 'tash' their good clothes with rain, I put on my best silver-grey fine woollen suit, my fur stole with its nosegay of roses, and a matching grey and turquoise hat.

'My Goad,' my mother said in despair. 'Look at her! Dressed as if she wis gaun tae a weddin' in her best claes, and it's poorin' wi' rain.'

'I don't care, Mother,' I said obstinately. 'It's the Queen's Coronation, and it's far more important than any wedding. I must look my best. I must be dressed for the occasion.'

'But she's no' likely tae *see* you!' said my mother. 'Your claes will get wasted. Pit oan a raincoat.'

'No,' I said.

On the way to the station we passed quiet, hurrying figures, all carrying baskets or cases with the day's food, for it would be a long wait, and there on the station platform was a poster announcing the glorious news that we had conquered the mighty Everest. Somehow it was just right to read such news on such a morning, and we talked of it in low eager tones as we travelled to town.

At Green Park the escalators had been put out of action to avoid accident, and we toiled laboriously upwards, the elderly pausing for breath halfway up, the youngsters racing to the top as fast as their legs could go.

A whole detachment of police and station officials sorted us out with the speed of an egg-counting machine, checking all tickets, and then we were in the Park, the cold raw air fanning our cheeks, a swift excitement mounting as we saw the stands on every side filling up, and the pavements packed with drowsy sightseers squatting on newspapers, groundsheets or shawls, most of whom had been there from the previous night.

Green Park was like a Sunday-school picnic on a gigantic scale. Tents, tarpaulins, temporary buildings, marquees, scores of refuse bins, stalls, all combined to transform its familiar appearance to something new and unfamiliar. To our amazement workmen were still erecting barriers and putting last-minute touches to the seating and the fences. We'd imagined everything would have been completed at least the night before.

Detachments of police were drilling, ready to take their places at various control points; St John Ambulance squads stood in groups waiting to move off. A couple lay fast asleep under a tree, the Coronation and the world forgot in their overmastering desire for rest.

The temporary canteens were doing a brisk trade, but we pressed on until we found the Equity stand, showed the precious tickets and went to find our seats. The first person I bumped into was our own Gordon Jackson, and with yells of 'Molly,' 'Gordon' we launched ourselves at each other, laughing with excitement to find a weel-kent Scots face among that huge assembly. Further along, up popped a lass with whom I'd worked in a schools' broadcast, in front of us was the actress with whom I'd played in Sunday repertory, behind was the Equity subscription secretary herself (another Scot), and alongside was an actor who'd been in a Lyons' show as a guest one week. It was all very warm and friendly, and somehow indescribably happy in spite of the grey skies.

We left our bags on the seats and decided to stroll across the Park to have a look at the Palace. Nothing would be happening in Piccadilly for hours, and we might as well see 'Buck House' where the Queen must at that minute be getting ready for the heavy day which lay ahead. We hadn't expected to do more than have a look, but that part of the Park was surprisingly free of crowds and we were able to stroll about and gaze at the wonderful mounted troops standing by to escort the carriages, and exclaim with excitement, 'Look, look, there are the children,' when a pointing finger alerted us all that Prince Charles and Princess Anne had their noses pressed to nursery windows as they watched the fascinating scene below.

As we strolled past a fenced enclosure we noticed several people on top of the wall behind the fence, obviously hoping for a glimpse of the procession as it went down the Mall. 'What a good idea,' I thought, and followed three ATS girls who'd squeezed through the fence in an attempt to get nearer to the wall and scramble to the top.

A patrolling commissionaire saw what was happening and yelled for police reinforcements! Before I knew it, I was clambering over the wall in the wake of the ATS girls, regardless of my best silk stockings, and running wildly in the opposite direction.

My better half, safely on the other side of the fence, shouted, 'Keep going, the police are after you!'

The instinct to run from the law must be strong within all of us, for I ran as if my life depended on it, and suddenly, to my surprise, I found myself in the press enclosure, exactly opposite Buckingham Palace, the entire pageant of gorgeously attired cavalry, Guards, troops and carriages almost under my nose. This was a far cry from a precarious perch on top of the wall I'd sought, and I was so overcome I completely forgot the pursuing police, and the outraged commissionaire, and only knew that I'd unwittingly arrived at one of the finest places on the Coronation route.

When the police arrived to check the tickets and ticket-holders in search for the fleeing interlopers, they took one look at my elegant outfit and passed me by, obviously inferring that such a fashionable female couldn't possibly have scrambled over a wall with the gatecrashers. Thank goodness I hadn't followed my mother's advice and worn a raincoat. I drew my fur stole closer around me, sniffed swooningly at my roses, and the moment of danger passed. Unfair, I know, but it isn't the first time an imposing front has saved the day! And anyway I didn't intend to stay where I was, I had a seat of my own somewhere.

And that's how it happened that I saw the Coronation procession leaving Buckingham Palace. I cheered myself hoarse, an Irishman on my left, and a Cockney on my right, all three of us gatecrashers. They'd been ejected during the police check, but had crept back during a lull, which I'd never have had the nerve to do, and our mingled accents rang out, wild with enthusiasm, the more so as we knew we had no right to be there.

We cheered the magnificent Queen Salote of Tonga who rode in an open carriage, dark head raised rapturously to the pouring rain, long arm held upright in salute. Rain is a sign of good luck in Tonga. A huge woman, over six feet tall, she caught the imagination of the crowd and was cheered to the echo.

Incidentally, I loved Noël Coward's *bon mot*, when somebody asked who the man was in the carriage beside Queen Salote.

'Her lunch,' replied Coward succinctly.

No prizes for guessing the island used to be cannibal!

When our own Queen left in her lovely coach, my next problem was to get out of this expensive £25 enclosure, for everyone was supposed to stay put there until the return journey, and I had no pass to get through the side door for I surely was not a member of the press and was not entitled to one.

So back over the fence it had to be and, miracle of miracles, Sandy suddenly appeared and caught me as I leaped from the high railing, and I didn't even ladder my stockings. Excitement had obviously turned me into an acrobat!

We raced back through the Park to our lawful places in the stand on the Piccadilly route, starving for a picnic lunch, early though it was, laughing and amazed at what we had so far accomplished. Sandy had seen a bit of the pageantry from the top of two biscuit tins, but he nobly rejoiced that I'd had such a wonderful view. 'You'll be able to describe it all much better than I could,' he said. 'And maybe even write about it some day.'

The loudspeakers kept us advised of everything that was happening at the Abbey, and now that everyone was in position and the officials could relax, a huge van drew up and lunch 'pokes' were distributed to the soldiers lining the route. This was good for a big cheer, and the lads ate their rolls somewhat self-consciously.

As we followed the service in the Abbey one of the most moving moments occurred when the thousands of spectators lining the route and in the stands rose in a single movement and joined in the singing of 'All People that on Earth do Dwell'. I had never thought to hear such a sound or witness such a sight in Piccadilly, one of the most sophisticated thoroughfares in the world. It was a wonderful moment.

Rain battered down intermittently, but a jolly crowd on the opposite pavement kept spirits soaring and laughter bubbling when they led us all in singing 'You are My Sunshine' and 'It Ain't Gonna Rain No More' and then, inevitably, 'Oh Why are We Waiting'.

Then at last the outriders came into view, and behind them the glitter, the gold, the procession, the colour, the thrilling amazing sight of thousands of magnificently turned out men of many nations, polished to the last button, filling Piccadilly as far as the eye could see. They told us there were twenty-nine thousand troops taking part. I would have believed them if they had said there had been a hundred thousand, it looked such an endless pattern of colour and movement.

I never thought to hear the Hampden roar in London, for the English are a reticent race, but the full-throated roar which greeted the first column of troops made my spine tingle. The Mounties were magnificent, the Guards a parade of toy soldiers, the Gurkhas had a cheer all to themselves, and their nut-brown faces broke into a brief smile as a wag yelled something in their own language. Fiji Islanders with their mops of black fuzzy hair and short skirts looked barbaric and dazzling, and the Marines, even among that meticulously drilled assembly, stood out with just that little bit extra which drew another full-throated roar from the crowd.

Then the Commonwealth ministers, and again Queen Salote in her open coach, Nehru in his little white hat, the Sultan of Johore splendid and mysterious, and all gazing with wonder and delight at our enthusiasm.

We had been warned we must not stand up in our places, except for the Queen's coach, for not only might it block others' views, it wan't too safe in such temporary stands. We had obeyed this order, apart from the earlier hymn-singing, but now the next carriage showed a hand out-thrust, the fingers raised in the V sign, the black velvet tammy of the Knight of the Garter just showing at the window, and we knew that here was the hero who had saved us in the war which was still so vivid in our memories.

Everything else was forgotten but that we must pay him homage and show him our love. It was like a great wave, this instant response to greatness. We rose, unmindful of orders, and our 'Hurrahs' to the Great Churchill drowned out every other sound, and sent a great flock of pigeons flying off in alarm.

Nobody told us to sit down.

We stared at each other, elation filling our shining eyes.

On this great day, we had actually seen Churchill.

It was £8 well spent for that moment alone.

Then there was a roar of sympathetic love and greeting for the Queen Mother and the bonnie Princess Margaret, and then the fairy coach with the marching escort in scarlet and gold and our dazzling young Queen inside, wearing her lovely crown and carrying the symbols of her office. Philip, resplendent in uniform, was smiling by her side. We were all on our feet now, cheering, yelling, waving, crying, tears streaming unashamed, lungs bursting, in our endeavour to show her how much we loved her, how much we admired her for the truly magnificent way she had played this long and difficult role before the biggest audience the world had ever known.

I felt glad to be among the acting fraternity, for we probably know better than anyone how nerves and tiredness can spoil a performance, and we knew we had watched a flawless performance.

A little girl beside us, daughter of an actress, said, 'Oh, Mummy, I saw the Queen, and I saw Philip and do you know what Philip said to me? He said, "Perhaps you'll come to tea one day." '

We laughed at her imaginative powers, but we needed no imagination to make the day perfect for us. We had seen something beyond the imagination of any of us and we were well content.

My mother had had a marvellous day too.

All the neighbours had come in, for nobody else in our lane had a TV set, and she'd had company all day. She was astounded by the length of the TV ceremonies. She'd thought the neighbours would just be in for about an hour, and could hardly believe it when they had made coffee, and handed round biscuits. Then they had disappeared for a quick lunch and rushed back again almost immediately, and had only gone back to their own houses before we arrived, about six o'clock in the evening.

After tea we watched the whole thing again on TV with our Australian relatives who'd been in London all day just to savour the atmosphere of the occasion. They had no seats, but they wanted to be able to tell their children, and their grandchildren that they had been in London on the day that Queen Elizabeth II had been crowned.

'My word,' laughed my mother. 'You're looking faur afore ye, thinking aboot grandweans already!'

But I knew what they meant.

It had been a great day to be in the capital, and although the TV account of the proceedings was enjoyable, and we saw right inside Westminster Abbey which we couldn't do from our seat in Piccadilly, still there was something indescribably moving and exciting to be actually part of the glory of the Coronation, and I for one would never forget it.

I took my mother up to London later in the week, and we visited St James's Palace where the robes and other royal trappings were on display. There was a separate window for the sale of entrance tickets for juveniles, and my mother and I were highly amused when the commissionaire directed me to that window! Clearly the years of playing schoolgirls were still stamped on my face!

But it was my mother who sent a ripple of laughter round the queue which snaked round the hall and up the tall staircase when she looked all round admiringly and said, 'I'll hiv tae whitewash the ceilings when I get hame. I wonder hoo they keep this place sae clean?'

She was very taken aback by the sight of very small boys in long trousers, which was not the custom in Glasgow at that time. Scottish children wore short trousers until they left school, and it was a sign that they were at last grown up when they went into what they called 'their longs'. She stopped dead in Bond Street when confronted by a wee boy about four years old, in immaculate grey flannels, trotting along quietly, holding his mother's hand.

'My,' said my mother in wonder, 'the wee boys here is awfu' like wee men.'

Ian Sadler, my Scottish actor friend from radio days in Glasgow, was convulsed by this remark when I repeated it to him and said he'd dine out on it for years, but I hoped the wee boy's mother didn't understand my mother's Scottish accent.

It was a revelation to see London through my mother's eyes. She noted things I had been blind to because I'd lived in the south for years. In the Tube she looked round and said in surprise, 'You never see ony weans in London, in thae trains, or buses.' It was true. Compared with Glasgow's trams and buses, which were thronged with people of all ages, from grannies to babes in arms, push-chairs and go-carts, London's transport seemed to carry a mainly adult population. And mostly youngish adults at that. And I'd never noticed it consciously before. I just accepted it as the London scene.

The housewives in Pinner intrigued her because they never seemed to wear workaday clothes for their housework and gardening. 'They're aye dressed,' she said to me somewhat disapprovingly, for she thought it very extravagant and wasteful to wear good clothes for humble tasks. She applauded my wearing an apron when baking or cleaning, even with my working slacks, for she couldn't endure spots or stains, and, like me, she'd never have felt dressed if she went up to the shops in the same clothes she'd worn to do the household chores.

Or maybe it should have been the other way round. Maybe I behaved like this, because I took my standards from her, and the grime of Glasgow dictated her habits.

She was getting to be quite a hardened traveller by this time, and although she loved Pinner she never wanted to stay longer than her holiday month. She knew I set aside this month to be with her every day, as far as I possibly could, and she wouldn't have enjoyed being alone if I were out in the studios and Sandy at the office. She couldn't understand the English 'twang' as she called it, and they found her very broad, although they were friendly and neighbourly in the street.

She could never get over the long hours the Londoners worked, for with the commuting added to the day's work Sandy used to leave the house in the mornings before eight o'clock, sometimes around seven-thirty a.m. and wasn't back at night until between six-thirty and seven p.m. 'Aye,' she'd say, 'it's a good job you've got your wireless work, for it wid be an awfu' long day here by yoursel' wi' Sandy bein' oot at his work a' that time.' This was a terrific acknowledgement, coming from her, for she always thought a man out at work deserved to have his wife at home to keep everything well run, and a good hot meal waiting for him at the end of the day. It was pleasant to feel that at long last she accepted me as a career woman.

And around this time my career took an unexpected twist. TV was now growing more popular, thanks to the Coronation when hundreds of people besides us had bought sets, and the programmes were getting better and more interesting by the week it seemed.

Panel games caught the public imagination, and people were glued to their sets to watch *What's My Line?*, with

Gilbert Harding, Lady Barnet, Barbara Kelly and Jerry Desmonde, among others who filled the seats as work exigencies dictated. Gilbert became the real draw of the programme and was on every week eventually, as were Lady Barnet and Barbara Kelly. It was a great 'shop window' and panellists became personalities overnight. Although we didn't realize it, TV was creating its own gods now.

Everybody wanted to be on *What's My Line?*.

Flushed with the success of this panel game, another was started, called *The Name's The Same*, with Frank Muir and Denis Norden, Brenda Bruce and Katie Boyle. Contestants with the same name as famous people from literature, history, art, sport, etc., presented themselves to the panel, who had to guess the connection and the name within twenty seconds of questioning. There was also a famous guest, hidden, who had to be guessed, and then *his* choice of famous ancestor had to be guessed too.

It took a trick immediately, and I longed to be in it. Everybody in show business tried to make an appointment with Brian Tesler, who did the casting for the panel games, and it was just about as impossible as angling for an appointment with the Queen! I'd rung umpteen times, but had had no luck in persuading him to see me.

Then one day, dressed to the nines to make a good impression, I went to the TV Centre, halfway across London from Pinner, to fulfil an arranged interview with another producer. When I reached his office, I found he'd had to dash out on an urgent assignment an hour or so earlier. His secretary was shattered because she'd forgotten to ring to let me know. She knew it had taken me at least an hour and a half to get to the Centre and, wishing to compensate for her oversight, this delightful girl asked me if there was anybody else I'd like to see.

Quick as lightning, seizing this golden opportunity, I said, 'Yes. Brian Tesler.'

She drew a quick breath.

'I'll see what I can do,' she promised, and rushed out of the office and along the corridor.

Now I didn't know that this young lady was a former secretary and trusted colleague of Brian's. It was my good luck that of all the females in the TV Centre I'd picked the only one who could have swung an appointment for me with the kingpin of panel games.

He agreed to see me for five minutes. And what valuable time that was! Straight away he fired half a dozen questions at me on the lines of the quiz he was working out for that evening. Shaking as I was, with dry tongue and hot face, I got every one of them right.

Later, Brian's secretary, who had been in the room at the time, told me I was the first person to be auditioned who had the slighest idea of what she was doing, or who gave anything like a performance.

It was probably the sheer unexpectedness of the opportunity which did it. I had no time to be devious, or to work out anything. It was partly intuition and partly knowledge, and there was no doubt Brian Tesler was impressed. I was promised the next opening. Which came much sooner than any of us in the room that afternoon could have guessed.

8

Within ten days of that unexpected audition in Brian Tesler's office the phone rang when I was getting ready to go into town for the Lyons' radio rehearsal. It was Tesler. 'Brenda Bruce is ill,' he said. 'She's had a dental operation and has a swollen jaw and a black eye. We want you to take her place.'

My stomach did about half a dozen somersaults, while I heard my voice asking about clothes, rehearsal times, and then telling him I'd have to finish my radio rehearsal first. This usually finished about eight o'clock. 'Ask them to let you away at seven tonight, Molly,' he said. 'This is a very important appearance for you, and I'm sure they'll not stand in your way.'

When I went into the rehearsal room, Richard was holding the *Evening News*, and he turned it round to show me a picture of myself on the front page. 'My God,' he said, 'I thought you'd dropped dead when I saw that photograph on the news-stands.' In the world of show business at that time the front page was reserved for the premature death of the public's idols!

Ben and Bebe were mildly interested in the fact that I was about to make my first appearance on TV in a panel game, but they were naturally much more concerned with our own radio script. I tried to calm my skittering heart, and cool my burning cheeks, and to concentrate with full attention on the show I was doing at that minute, which was playing Aggie in *Life with the Lyons*. I had ascertained that I could get away around seven o'clock, and I was too wise to ask again, and give the impression that I was skipping my work and dying to leave.

The clock crept round to seven o'clock – we were in the middle of another run-through and could easily go on till half past. And I had to get from Bond Street to Shepherd's Bush, a good half-hour's journey by Tube. The TV show, which was done live of course, went on the air around nine, and before then I must be made up, have my hair done, change into evening dress, and have a dummy rehearsal with the regulars. But if I never got there I wasn't going to precipitate any arguments by clock-watching. I turned my back to the big timepiece on the wall and went steadily on with the script, rising when it was my turn to speak, and moving back when it wasn't. It was probably the best acting I'd done for a long time, this assumption of calm concentration when everything inside me was jumping about like a firecracker!

Bebe, as always, was absorbed in the script to the exclusion of everything else. Ben studiously ignored the time, half teasing, half serious, for he rightly felt our show came first. When the clock showed a quarter past seven Richard said, 'Daddy, you'd better let Aggie go. She hasn't anything else in the script and she doesn't have to wait for notes. She can get them tomorrow.' I could have hugged him – dear, dear Richard, always aware of everyone's difficulties.

Ben looked up in feigned surprise. 'Oh yeah,' he said. 'You wanted to get away. Where have you got to go?'

'Lime Grove, in Shepherd's Bush,' I said, carelessly, as though it were just round the corner.

'Oh well, you'd better get off then,' said Ben. 'You're on tonight, aren't you?'

Was I not!

'Are you sure you're finished with me?' I asked, as though it didn't matter in the least when I left.

'Go on,' Ben roared, 'before I change my mind!'

I collected my things, including the little case with my blue velvet evening dress, walked demurely from the room, and then went like a bat out of hell the minute I was out of the door. I rushed to the Tube station, fell into the train, and was soon whirling to Lime Grove.

I was practically sick with fright by this time. *The Name's The Same* was entirely different from the game in which I'd done so well in Tesler's office. Every London newspaper had featured me on its front page, and people going home were reading 'Aggie steps in for Brenda', 'Scots girl in top panel game', 'The face behind the voice'. At that moment the face behind the voice was blenched with sheer blind panic.

When I got to Lime Grove, everybody was waiting to go through a 'dry run', with fictitious names to guess, just to see how the 'new girl' fitted in. I found I was guessing so hard and worrying so much about categories that I wasn't listening to what the others in the team were saying, and so I was wasting questions on information they had already received. Oh gosh, I was going to make a right mess of it and fall flat on my face in front of millions of viewers, not to mention a live audience in the theatre. Brian Tesler didn't look too happy either!

By the time Katie Boyle and I went along to have our hair done and our faces made up, my nerves were stretched to breaking point. Frank Muir and Denis Norden strolled in to wish me luck, cool as cucumbers, and I wondered how I had ever dared even to *want* to be in a panel game, and to pit my wits alongside such established top-rank players as those two brilliant chaps. If I never knew it before, I now knew that there was only one thing worse than not getting what you want and that was getting it.

Katie was sweet and friendly and told me not to worry. It was all very well for her, she'd been playing this game for months. I could see she was nervous all the same, but it was a sort of controlled nervousness compared with my palsied fright. She looked gorgeous with her rose-leaf complexion and perfect teeth, and very attractive hair. I had the comfort at least of knowing that on that score I looked reasonably presentable myself in my favourite midnight blue velvet evening dress, sparkly ear-rings (they were a great eye-catching talking point with all lady panellists!) and an effective hair-do.

A young man came and collected us to take us through to the theatre, carefully making sure we saw none of the contestants, who'd been smuggled into their rooms while we were busy with our 'glamorizing' treatment.

We were introduced to the audience and shown to our seats behind the narrow table, pads and pencils in readiness for any notes, carafes and glasses to attend to our thirst, if required.

Denis Norden was seated at the far end of the table. Next to him came Katie, next to her Frank, and I was right at the end, nearest to the audience, so I needn't face them when I was doing my questioning, for the contestants would sit across from us, slightly upstage.

My legs had been trembling, but suddenly as we went on the air my fears completely vanished and a tremendous excitement and concentration took their place. I forgot the audience, both at home and out there in the theatre. I seemed to have all the time in the world to ask questions, and I scored four correct answers, with mounting excitement from the audience. It was a gift from God to be so lucky for my first-ever appearance in such a show, and the

Lyons were ecstatic with 'Aggie's' success. They phoned the minute we were off the air, and somehow that was almost the most surprising thing about that unforgettable evening, that they knew and were able to get right through to speak to me at Lime Grove. I never ceased to be surprised at the ease with which VIPs could cut straight through red tape, without let or hindrance.

Sandy was quietly proud that I'd not let the side down, and told me I looked very good on the screen.

The newspapers next day were filled with extravagant praise. The 'face behind the voice' had been a wow! I had looked as if I was genuinely enjoying myself. I had played it as a game, and not as a matter of life and death! Little did they know the terrors I'd endured beforehand! Not a word of poor Brenda Bruce, whose illness had given me my chance. I dropped her a note to wish her well, for truly her misfortune had been my lucky break.

Almost immediately after this excitement had died down, I had a phone call from the TV people in Glasgow BBC. Their first question took me by surprise. 'Have you ever ridden a horse?' they queried.

I laughed. 'Well, we do have a Rotten Row in Glasgow which was once my home town, but it's not noted for horse-riding skills!'

'Come on, come on,' the voice said. 'Have you ever taken part in any horse-riding activities?'

'Not me,' I said. 'The only horse I know is the milkman's.'

They were delighted. They wanted to present me on Easter Sunday afternoon, from Gleneagles, as a beginner at pony-trekking who had never handled a horse before. I was to be a pupil guinea-pig taking elementary instruction in the handling, saddling and riding of a pony of the type used in pony-trekking, all before the cameras, with complete honesty, and no rehearsing.

We'd been planning a holiday ourselves for that Easter, so I determined that Sandy must share the pleasure of a location in such a desirable spot as Gleneagles. As a golfer he'd be in his element!

The BBC agreed to make it a double booking, and we'd pay the difference ourselves. I may say that Sandy has considered this the best 'perk' we ever had.

Clothes were no problem, fortunately, for I was booked at fairly short notice. I had a scarlet suit at that time, and the jacket was a dead ringer for hunting 'pink', and worn with black trousers and my hair tied back in a pony-tail was neat and eye-catching for such a programme.

I wasn't allowed to touch the horse before the show. A young lad was engaged as a stand-in for me during the rehearsals which were essential for camera line-up, positions, and other technical considerations. I had merely to stand by, watching the moves, so that I'd know what was expected of me. There was no dialogue. It was back to the Blackpool sketch, with me making up the lines as I went along. But this time the pony wouldn't be able to answer back!

My one fear was that when I came to work with the beast it might suddenly jerk its head and hit me in the face. They pooh-poohed my fears. 'It's most unlikely,' they said.

Just to prove them wrong and confirm my direst forebodings, at the end of the rehearsal the pony suddenly reared its head and hit the boy full in the face. There was no time to duck, although this lad was very experienced with animals, and he went down with blood pouring down his face.

I went to bed that night, seeing nothing but that unconscious blood-daubed face!

'I can't do it,' was my last thought, before I fell asleep. 'I'm sure to get my nose broken.'

Sandy, who'd been playing golf all day on the famous

course, having been adopted as a member of the team, all of whom had been given the freedom of the course, was so ecstatic over his golf that he dismissed my fears with a laugh. 'Just as every dog is allowed one bite, maybe every pony is allowed to blood one nose, and he's had his dunt,' he said. 'You'll be all right, hen.'

Henry Hall was playing at the hotel, and he walked round with me, and we were photographed together near the field where the action was to be. He too was quite sure I'd be a wow, and I began to tell myself I was daft to be so worried, for it was a glorious day in Scotland and nobody would be so silly as to sit indoors on a lovely Easter Sunday. Nobody would be watching. It might have infuriated the organizers to know that I had every confidence we'd be playing to empty rooms, but it surely was a great comfort to me.

What I hadn't taken into consideration at all was the weather in England, where I discovered later it had pelted with rain all day.

As a result, millions of stay-at-home Bank Holiday viewers, whose numbers I never suspected, were enchanted to be taken by proxy to Gleneagles and watch my antics with Islay, the white pony. I lifted the pony's mane and played peek-a-boo behind it. I ran my hands up and down its legs and apologized for my familiarity. I lifted its tail and turned my face away delicately. I finally got on to its back, with the cry, 'Heigh-ho, Silver', and then as it moved forward called out, 'Look, Ma, I'm riding,' and then, 'Look – no hands!'

I was giving such a crazy performance that I forgot all about the possibility of being hit on the face, and dear little Islay behaved like a perfect lady and left me unbloodied and unbowed. I could see Henry Hall doubled up with laughter as I left the field, and Sandy said it had been very funny.

One delighted viewer was my wee nephew in Glasgow.

His mother told me afterwards that he had been so enthralled that when other ponies moved in front of the camera and blotted me out on the screen, he had yelled, 'Hey, get awa' oot o' it! I want to see ma auntie on a horse.'

All that clowning, which I was sure nobody would see, brought me the biggest fan-mail since *ITMA*. And the press were full of enthusiasm. One newspaper, after describing my 'correct' outfit, described my introduction to horseflesh for the first time as absolutely hilarious, and even quoted my spur-of-the-moment dialogue with Islay – 'It's all right, it's your Auntie Molly, son . . . hen,' when the beast grew restless, and, at my attempt to put the bit in its mouth, 'Don't take a wee bite now, pet, I need both my hands.' Another flatteringly declared it would be an excellent idea to make it a series, with me as the comical pupil learning skiing, yachting and fishing! Somehow I think I was a lot safer with the pony.

Now that it was all over, and I had survived unscathed, I could bask in the approval which came my way, and I heard later that thanks to our TV riding lesson the pony-trekking season was assured of success, for they'd had hundreds of applications for that type of holiday that summer.

As for Sandy, that glorious, golden weekend on one of the world's finest golf-courses became a treasured memory, and made up for a lot of the tedious hours which seemed inevitable in being married to a busy actress.

When we got back to London, we heard that Brenda Bruce was going into a London play, and I was booked to take her place regularly in *The Name's The Same*. Again the newspapers practically gave me a nervous breakdown with all their enthusiastic advance publicity. Headlines proclaimed 'Tattie takes over from Brenda tonight' – this from somebody who obviously remembered me more vividly from *ITMA* than from *Life with the Lyons*. Another said, 'Enter Molly, the lass with the nimble pencil' – this in reference to my high speed shorthand-writing. A third said, 'Calling on Aggie', and they were all quite, quite sure that I was going to repeat my dazzling performance on my first appearance!

I wasn't! And I didn't!

It's one thing making a single appearance when the significance of the occasion heightens perception, when all the signals are obvious, and when the whole thing falls into place like a jigsaw; it's quite another taking part week by week, and having to work whether or not one is tired, excited, fuzzy with a cold, or just plain uninspired.

There were only a few weeks of the series to run, and, luckily I fitted in well enough to please them all, although I never repeated my first phenomenal four right guesses. But I had become enough of a draw to be booked for the panel game which succeeded *The Name's The Same*. This was *One of the Family* and the contestants were actually truly related to some famous ancestor whom they'd successfully traced through the family tree.

Again we had to elicit the relationship and name by questioning, and I was never far from my *Dictionary of Famous Names* once this show got under way. Knowing nothing whatsoever about cricket, I studied the cricket stars and their performances and became so adept at pinpointing a particular player that my dressmaker's husband, a cricket enthusiast, gained a new respect for my intelligence! 'But I know nothing about it,' I protested. 'I just memorize all their names.' And so I did.

I was soon having it said, even by the producer, that I had the second sight. 'Look, Molly,' said Brian, 'we don't want genius. We just want ordinary intelligence. If you guess at that speed, we'll run out of names.'

The public began to call me 'Psychic Clara', and the viewing figures rose as people tuned in to see how accurate I'd be. I can't offer any explanation. Paul Jennings said it wasn't skill, it was sheer feminine intuition. I think he was right.

I only know that some nights a power of intuition seemed to possess me. When I was 'on the beam' at such times, I could guess the challengers' names as though they were written in letters of fire above their heads.

When I was off form, I couldn't have got them if they'd shouted them aloud letter by letter.

That's when perspiration had to take over from inspiration, and Sandy always said I was much funnier when I couldn't guess a thing, and much less like an examining counsel!

We had a celebrity spot on this programme, just as we had in *The Name's The Same*, and not only had we to guess the celebrity but we had also to guess who he'd have preferred to have been.

Henry Hall told me he was absolutely certain I had second sight, because he'd chosen someone he thought nobody could possibly guess. But I guessed it in seconds. 'If you weren't Henry Hall, I think you'd have liked to have been Confucius.' He couldn't get over it.

With Denis Compton it was not intuition but sheer deduction which gave me the answer. I took a long look at the great cricketer, speculated that though he seemed a quiet relaxed man, the right sort to enjoy such a slow game, his eyes revealed a liveliness which could have meant a desire for speed. When I confirmed this with my first question, I then went on to discover that it was speed in the air he craved, and it just had to be Neville Duke. Every time I see Denis he reminds me of that.

One of the side-effects of all this panel-game popularity

was that I began to be recognized everywhere I went. No more blessed anonymity. No more skipping around the village or London in workaday clothes. I was seized upon by complete strangers, and shaken by the hand, and told how much they enjoyed me on TV. Or hadn't enjoyed me!

And I had an amusing, or embarrassing, demonstration that, no matter what I wore, recognition would come my way. We were on holiday in Ireland, and I went along to the toilet in the train, and found when I tried to get out again that the lock had given up the ghost and fallen to the floor, leaving the bolt firmly wedged into the door-frame. I was trapped! I banged and yelled and kicked the door, but not a sound could be heard over the rattle of the train. Finally Sandy came in search of me, as I'd been absent so long, and although I didn't know what was happening, he'd found the guard, who came along with a screwdriver, and released me.

I was so embarrassed, for the corridor was packed by this time with interested passengers, that I decided to make a joke of it, and I fell out into the guard's arms, crying, 'Trapped in the toilet! And mercifully released in the nick of time!'

As soon as he clapped eyes on me, the guard shouted, 'It's the wee Scots lass from the Telly. Tell me, miss, how do ye guess all thim fellas the way ye do?'

I was absolutely astounded at such instant recognition, for I was dressed in cycling jeans, thick pullover, had my hair tied back in a pony-tail and, for good measure, my lips and nose were festooned with the ugly herpes which strong sea air always brings out. And yet this Irish guard, who had only ever seen me in full TV make-up, dressed in silks and velvets and adorned with diamanté ear-rings, hadn't the slightest difficulty in recognizing me. So much for glamour!

The panel games had rocketed me so swiftly and so surely into the limelight of instant recognition as a celebrity that I found it almost incredible that only a brief three or four years earlier I had felt isolated and far from home because I didn't know a living soul apart from my own dear Sandy in our Pinner village.

Now I couldn't go into a bus without everybody from the conductor to the lady in the seat beside me calling out, 'It's Molly', or 'It's Aggie', or, 'How do you get on with Gilbert Harding then?' Everybody mixed up the panel games and were always asking me about Gilbert, with whom I had never worked at that time. As it would have taken too long to put them right, I just smiled amiably, as I did when people were convinced I actually lived with the Lyons and murmured, 'Oh, I get on very well. His bark is worse than his bite.'

When I stopped to ask the way one day in Hammersmith the two milkmen I'd approached for directions grinned and said, 'On your way to Lime Grove, Aggie? That was a good show you did last week.'

A Euston chemist looked at me shrewdly when I went in to buy a packet of glucose. 'Oh, is that where you get all your sparkle on TV?' she murmured as she handed me my change.

Shopping anywhere now took twice as long, for every shop I entered offered a post mortem not only on the last show I'd done but on every single show on TV. Everybody had his comment to make, and his advice to offer. Charlie Chester used to be amazed and infuriated by the public's cheek in appointing themselves outspoken critics of things they knew little about. Charlie used to wonder what the painter or the plumber would say if he came and inspected their work and offered his advice unasked.

I'm one of those actresses who likes to dress to the

weather, irrespective of glamour. If it's a wet day I like a raincoat. If it's cold I like a heavy coat, and if the sun shines I like a sundress and sandals. If my hair is a mess I like to tie it back or put it up under a scarf, and I've been known to keep on a pair of tights which have laddered for an entire day.

When I was on sound radio I could indulge this preference for ordinary behaviour without anyone thinking any the less of me, but after TV popularity entered my unsuspecting life I found myself on view every time I stepped outside our own front door, and had to be prepared to be scrutinized from top to toe. Like the soldier in danger of bumping into an MP round every corner, I was always on parade.

I smiled wryly when a friend, a famous TV personality, told me he was going to a remote corner of Europe for his holiday to escape this merciless scrutiny. 'Think of it, Molly,' he exulted, 'I can *limp* if I want to! And if my nose is itchy I can make a face, and squint to see if there's a hair on it.' Being under the limelight all the time had made such simple little freedoms beyond price to him.

For me it took quite a while to grow used to the extra-ordinary reactions of people whenever they caught sight of me, and the impression they gave that they truly felt they were real friends of mine. They'd come up to me and greet me and tell me their life story at the drop of a hat.

One day, when I directed a woman to a bus, she clutched my arm like a drowning creature when she realized I was Molly Weir of the Telly. 'Oh, wait till I tell my little girl, she won't go to bed until she's heard your laugh.' I learned in the next five minutes that she used to live in the south of England, that her husband had lost all his money trying to run a garage, had taken another job in London, that she was in rooms which cost her five guineas a week (a lot of money then), that her little girl was a fine lass, very clever at school, and that she would really have to take a part-time job to help to pay that iniquitous rent.

All this was gasped out practically in one breath, and it was obvious to me that she was starved of a sympathetic ear in her strange new environment, and that mine was the only weel-kent face she'd seen for a long, long time, and she assumed I'd be interested in her troubles. I was, very, if only I hadn't had the un-Christian feeling that I was going to be late for my next appointment, and I'd never seen the poor soul in my life before and probably wouldn't see her again. But I think I did her a bit of good, for she left me looking much happier, and with a tale to tell to her wee girl. I'd just have to tell a taller tale to the producer I'd kept waiting!

Another lady who spied me waiting for my train on my way from a distant rehearsal, came rushing up and told me her wee girl was really smart for six, for she'd spotted me right away from the far end of the platform, and knew I was Molly from the Telly. Within the next few minutes before the train came in, I heard how her husband had deserted her and had gone back to his mother, taking the Telly with him. So now they had to go to neighbours to see me! When I sympathized over his heartless behaviour in leaving her alone with her child, she said, 'Oh, I don't know. I was getting a bit fed up with him – but I do miss the Telly.'

I'll bet she didn't say that to the divorce court judge!

Even policemen of whom I asked the way ended up by asking *me* what it was like working with the Lyons.

Workmen, paid by us by the hour, stood idle in our kitchen as they questioned me avidly as to what it's like to be on Telly, and 'What's Eamonn Andrews really like?'

I remember Pat Hayes telling me that she thought then, seeing me on the receiving end of such dazzling acclaim for my panel performances, that I was at last on my way to the dizzy heights of real stardom. Pat herself was later to take the top award for her magnificent performance on TV as Edna in *Edna, the Inebriate Woman*. Pat and I were great friends, having worked together a lot on *Children's Hour*, and she was very sensible, and down-to-earth, and realistic in her assessments.

I'm glad she didn't tell me her predictions at the time, or my disappointment would have been all the greater when the whole bubble burst, and everybody grew tired of panel games overnight, it seemed. The newspapers, who had been so generous with their praise, now sniffed disparagingly. 'Actress Molly Weir, having suitably toned down her Scottish accent' (what cheek! I hadn't) 'has put a faint spark of life into wearisome panel games, with her amazing gift for long-shot answers. Unfortunately, the games are so much the same each week, that even the panel seems tired of participating.'

Well, that was telling us.

Not only was it telling us, it was telling the public, and it was telling the powers-that-be who hired and fired us.

When *One of the Family* ended its run it did not return. And, as far as I was concerned, that was the end of panel games and 'Psychic Clara'.

But although it had been a heady brew to be accepted as a draw in my own right, in contrast to being a small supporting cog in shows where the real draw was the big star, I accepted the end of this period philosophically. I had had the great good fortune to be brought up in a household where children weren't spoilt. Grannie and my mother had made us realize life was hard, and we must be prepared in every way to face it, and that sort of background has proved a bulwark against the inevitable blows and disappointments one has to face in show business.

And on the credit side, panel games may have ended, but I was now recognized in radio and on TV as a solo performer, as well as enjoying the continuing fun and work as Aggie in *Life with the Lyons*.

And, thanks to the *One of the Family* game, I had found a friend in Franklin Engelmann, who took over as chairman when Leslie Mitchell had had to leave due to ill-health.

Leslie Mitchell was 'front man' on so many programmes on TV at that time that his face was as well known as the lion in the MGM opening shot for all their films, or the cock crowing in *Topical Budget* which gave us the latest news when we went to the cinema. Everything about him was of interest, and when he appeared on our first programme with a poisoned eye, which necessitated his wearing a black patch over it, the critics were delighted to point out that it gave him a sinister touch, but that he still managed to retain his dignity and to give the programme pace.

I found he had a dry humour which delighted me, and I remember he had come to that first performance straight from Earls Court where he'd been doing the commentary on the Cattle Show. 'So nice to find there are people in the world again,' he said contentedly. 'I've been with bullocks and cows all day. I'd forgotten people existed.'

When he saw me twist round on my make-up chair to pick up a ribbon which had fallen he shut his eyes and grimaced with mock-pain. 'Oh don't *do* that, Molly!' he implored.

'Do what?' I asked in surprise.

'Don't twist your body like that, you've no idea how easily you can put a disc out.'

It was the first time I'd heard of the agonies of a slipped disc, and Leslie had suffered from this misery for years. It had all started with his bending over just as I had, with an awkward sideways movement, to pick up a book, and he'd seldom been free from pain since. He had to wear a steel corset all the time. That was another thing I'd not heard of. I stared at him with mounting respect. He was one more example of performers working under difficulties the public never suspected. And he kept smiling, and was pleasant and relaxed and professional in all circumstances in spite of the exhausting effects of a back which was seldom free from discomfort. No wonder one reads of actors giving a performance one night, and dropping dead the next! They do, literally, work till they drop. And it's not just that 'the show must go on' for traditional reasons. It must, because it is an inner compulsion, which cannot be denied.

But even the brave Leslie had to give up when hospital treatment became imperative, and in stepped Franklin Engelmann, or 'Jingle' as he was better known.

Handsome, courteous, and very humorous, we hit it off immediately, and he used to drop me off home on the way back from the studios after we'd done our TV show, for he lived not too far from Pinner. It wasn't long before we were invited to his home for dinner, and soon he and his wife Tynee, and Sandy and I were enjoying a very happy friendship.

I was most intrigued by Tynee's name and found out later that she'd been Jingle's driver when he went overseas as a war correspondent in the army. When they went to collect their mail, names were called out according to surname, with the Christian initials added, so when it came to her name the chap on postal duties would call out 'Tyne, E. E.', for her name was in fact Erica E. Tyne. And that's how she became known to Jingle, by a nickname spelt Tynee and not the 'Tinie' I'd been seeing in my mind's eye. No wonder I couldn't make 'Tinie' fit, for she was tallish and blonde, and not a wee smout like me!

He was the first actor who really got to know Sandy, and

to appreciate his wit. Sandy is quiet, but has a swift witty sense, and is far better read than I am. Jingle used to warm my heart when Sandy would come out with something funny and swiftly apropos to the subject under discussion, for he would throw his head back with laughter and then gasp, 'Oh, Sandy, I *wish* I had said that!'

This was a very nice, generous touch from a professional front man who always had to have the right word at the right time.

So when the panel games came to an end it certainly wasn't the end of seeing Jingle.

And it wasn't the end of solo appearances, for the TV people began using me as a storyteller, as a singer on afternoon revues, once even with our tandem bicycle as a freewheeling holiday-maker, and then in a most enjoyable daytime women's programme called *Domestic Forum* where I was the Jill-of-all-trades.

The tandem appearance was of most interest to Sandy, for he loved our bicycling holidays and he had a great affection for the old machine. The BBC sent a huge van to our house to collect it and transport it to Lime Grove, and Sandy had provided a negative of us cycling through Brittany which they projected on to the screen behind me as I stood leaning on the tandem.

I then told of our holiday and all the adventures we'd enjoyed, and of our food and clothing, and all the necessary preparations, and the cost of such a holiday. I'd written the script with blood, sweat, toil and tears. It seemed easy, but it took *seven* scripts to get it all to the right length, the right contents, and to have the right appeal for everyone who had to approve it.

It was put out live, as were most shows then, and Sandy nipped out of the office in the middle of the afternoon and sped into a TV shop in the City, to ask the owner if he could be allowed to look at *Holiday Hour*, as his wife was appearing in it.

'Blimey,' said the man. 'Don't you see enough of her? I wouldn't move to the end of the shop to see my old woman. Glad to get away from her, I am.'

Apologetically, Sandy explained that the tandem would also be appearing, as would also one of his photographs. 'Oh, that's different, guv,' the chap said. 'Wot time did you say it was on?'

Men!

Anyway, what with his golf at Gleneagles and now the old tandem and his photograph 'starring' in a programme, Sandy was beginning to feel TV was proving to be a very lively interest indeed in his life.

He never stopped telling me that if it hadn't been for his enthusiasm in acquiring a set I'd never have known what sort of shows were on, or what sort of work I could usefully do in that medium.

I had to admit he was right.

Considering what TV work lay ahead, it was strange to reflect that I had resisted it so strongly in the beginning.

9

The TV *Domestic Forum* series for afternoon viewing by women was a completely different cup of tea for me. The three other panellists were experts in their own field: Ruth Drew qualified in Domestic Science subjects, Frances Perry in gardening, Rosemary McRobert in Electricity Board matters plus consumers' interests, and I was the commonsensical housewife, with practical knowledge of cooking, cleaning, gardening, and running a house.

Viewers sent in questions, and we had to solve all their problems. We took it in turns to be chairman, and on such occasions had to decide who answered which question, time allocated, and whether it was the sort of question to be thrown open to general discussion. Specialist questions were dealt with, as far as possible, by the specialists involved, unless a commonsense answer which had been proved practically seemed more helpful and easier for the viewer to understand.

It was enormously interesting, and we often found ourselves debating hotly on the workable solutions to all sorts of problems we ourselves had experienced, and solved in quite a different way to that recommended by 'experts'.

It was very lively, and I became firm friends with all the panellists, and although I enjoyed our adlib chatter, I liked it less when I was chairman, which I found rather intimidating, with its insistence on strict time schedules and a brisk rounding up to get on with the next problem.

Ruth Drew was absolutely marvellous in the chair, and I always relaxed when she was in command, leaving the whole thing in her capable hands, and thankful I had merely to deal with questions. Until the awful afternoon when she had a message from the producer hissed into her ear during the programme: 'Go to question twenty after this one.'

Ruth in turn hissed into my ear, while the camera was on Rosemary McRobert, 'Carry on talking when I move to you, Molly. I don't know what question twenty is.'

We learned later that poor Ruth, imagining she was being terribly businesslike, had retyped all the questions on separate postcards, for ease in handling, but she had not put the question numbers on her cards! Her spectacles were in her handbag, and she had to scrabble about on the floor to find *them*, then find the producer's script and go frantically all through the dozen or so pages, to find question twenty, and, having found what it referred to, go through her cards to see what problem it concerned!

Meantime the camera had swung to me, and the moment Ruth had said, 'Well, Molly, what views do you have about this stained raincoat?' she dived to the floor for her handbag and her specs.

Normally we three others were allocated about five minutes or at the most six in total for dealing with each problem, so we had about one and a half to two minutes each. On this ghastly afternoon I found myself prattling for a full *five* minutes on my own! I discussed the fabric of the coat, the texture, and the colour. The various methods of removing stains from everything from carpets to evening gowns! I went into the advantages of dry cleaning over wet cleaning, the prices charged by various types of shops, providing varying services. I even went on to a wildly fictitious visit to an establishment which I described in my nervous babbling as 'one of the best-known rain-makers in the country'. Only a snort of suppressed laughter from the stunned Rosemary McRobert alerted me to what I'd said, and I laughingly interjected, 'Well, I didn't really consult a witchdoctor, it was a prosaic raincoat-maker actually!'

And *still* I had no signal that Ruth had found that elusive question twenty.

The camera seemed as hypnotized as the other three and made no attempt to move from my face. Just when I was on the point of collapsing from shortness of breath, never mind exhaustion of ideas, Ruth smiled radiantly, waved the card, and the camera picked her up. 'Now we will go on to question twenty, which is from a viewer in Bromley who would like to know about pulping apples.'

At the end of the programme we all fell about in hysterical laughter. Ruth said gratefully, 'Only somebody as talkative as Molly could have carried on all that time without a pause, and actually made sense.'

Rosemary was still giggling over the 'best-known rain-maker', and Frances stared at me admiringly, full of praise for my presence of mind and thankfulness she hadn't been asked to perform such a marathon. The joke of it was that I've never had any expertise in removing stains, and I have never at any time given myself even modest marks for my skills as a laundress.

Next day I met a neighbour at the shops, and she said, 'By Jove, that man who sent in the question about his stained raincoat must have been pretty pleased. I've never heard a question dealt with so thoroughly. Why did they give it all to you? I didn't realize you were such an expert!'

'Oh well,' I said, 'Ruth was in the chair, you see, and just passed it on to me as she had enough to do dealing with the questions and their allocation.' Ahem!

The programme took a break in the summer. It also occasionally varied the panel members, according to the degree of expertise required by some of the questions, so I found myself not required for the September programme, which was to see the start of the autumn schedules, and Sandy and I decided to fulfil a long-held ambition and spend our holiday in Yugoslavia. It had been the dream of my childhood fantasies to sail down the Adriatic, and as I do not like flying we had booked to go by train right through to Rijeka, and sail down the beautiful coast on the twenty-four-hour trip to Dubrovnik.

We could only book at the last minute, due to my unpredictable professional commitments, and hadn't been able to get a seaside hotel, but one in the town, the Hotel Imperial.

'Och well,' I'd said to Sandy, 'as this is such a late holiday, maybe we'll be just as well to be in the centre of things, and the weather might be awful, and grey sees aren't too enticing.' I was really just making the best of things, for I'm not fond of a noisy city bustle when on holiday, but as events turned out we couldn't have done better if that had been our first choice.

The day before we were due to leave, the phone rang. It was the BBC producer of *Domestic Forum*. 'Oh, Molly, Ruth asked me to ask you first. She is not very well, and she can't do tomorrow's programme and she wondered if you would stand in for her.'

'Anne,' I cried, 'I can't. We're due to leave for Yugoslavia in the morning, and everything has been booked right through, boats, sleepers, the lot, for we don't fly, and I just couldn't ask my husband to change his office arrangements at the last minute like this.'

I hated not being able to help Ruth, especially as she'd asked for me as her substitute, for she knew I would have done it without a moment's thought. I never minded being a substitute for anybody, and indeed often found the most exciting challenges were offered by such work. But we'd had to change holiday plans so often because of last-minute offers, causing all sorts of office dramas for poor Sandy and his colleagues, that I simply couldn't greet him with the news that Yugoslavia was off because a colleague was sick.

Anne tried to reassure me that she understood perfectly, and so would Ruth. And she repeated, 'I came to you first because Ruth said she could rely on you to step in if it was humanly possible.'

I felt terrible, but when Sandy came home he said, 'You're not the only one in that programme – they'll get somebody else only too easily. You did the right thing refusing. I certainly couldn't change my holidays again at this stage.'

So off we went, and the sail down the Adriatic was all that we could have dreamed of, and more! It was a Yugoslav ship, and the only language the crew spoke, apart from their own unintelligible (to us!) Serbo-Croat, was German. They looked more like Russians, and the food was strange but enjoyable, while the ship was new and clean as a new pin. There were only about half a dozen British on board, all the rest being Yugoslav or German or Scandinavian. We left Rijeka with the sun shining and the skies a deep beautiful blue, but when darkness fell thunder and lightning was raging, and crackling up and down the metal parts of the ship like fireworks. Blinding flashes lit up the shores, and revealed for seconds little villages. The sea boiled and roared, and it was one of the most exciting trips of a lifetime. Not frightening, somehow. Just exciting, like a colourful, noisy opera, with the storm doing the orchestration.

As we drew near Dubrovnik in pitch darkness someone called from a nearby ship, and the language sounded so much like the dialogue taught to me by Fred Yule for our speech in Tomptopia, that mythical country invented for us for *ITMA*, that on impulse I called back in loud tones, 'Awa-choo-choo-kay-kay-la-ba-ba,' my remembered comment in the land of Tomptopia.

A murmur of admiration rose from those standing near to us, who were convinced I was an expert in Serbo-Croat and had replied to the unseen caller in his own language!

Sandy and I had a job to stifle our laughter. For a quiet man I must say he took my wild extrovert behaviour amazingly calmly.

Dubrovnik was as black as the darkest tunnel, with not a light anywhere. I couldn't understand it, as we whirled through street after street in Stygian gloom, and thought it was possibly because Iron Curtain countries were so short of power that they didn't have street lighting. And it was only when we reached our hotel, which was also in complete darkness, with candles being lit as quickly as possible to sign us in, that it dawned on me that the storm had damaged the electricity supply, and that we had doubtless passed umpteen buildings all blacked out as we drove through the streets, buildings which of course were quite invisible to us in the darkness. So it hadn't been empty countryside after all, but a city whose brightness had been temporarily dimmed.

The Hotel Imperial was gorgeous. It had once been the Imperial Palace and we had a bedroom which would have held almost our entire house in Pinner. It even boasted a table as large as our dining table at home, but because of the proportions of the room it was dwarfed to the size of a coffee table. We had taken a box of Black Magic chocolates with us, having been warned sweets would be both scarce and expensive, and we used to sit ceremoniously at this large table each night at bedtime, and solemnly allow ourselves to consume one chocolate apiece! We'd counted them, and this was the only way to make sure that they'd last for the duration of the holiday.

We found the Yugoslavs were quiet, and tall and dignified, with no cheap gimmicks for the tourists. We bathed off the rocks a short way from the hotel, having found that the seaside sand was practically non-existent and not worth the trouble to reach. As the water was very deep, and I am not a very brave or strong swimmer, I wore a rubber ring to keep me afloat and to give confidence to my childish breaststroke. One day, when Sandy was swimming afar off, I found myself surrounded by a dozen male swimmers, rather like a school of whales surrounding a minnow. They were staring at me with a mixture of pity and amazement. '*Können Sie nicht schwimmen?*', one called to me anxiously, pointing to the rubber ring. '*Ja.*' I answered, patting the ring, '*Aber das ist besser!*'

I was rather proud of this little exchange in German, while paddling around like a duck, but Sandy, seeing the commotion, thought the ring had burst and that I was being rescued from drowning. He always said I had far too much confidence in the magic properties of that ring, and that one day I'd find out it wasn't indestructible and I'd sink like a stone if he wasn't nearby. However, all was well on this occasion, although he'd broken his own speed swimming record to reach me to find this out!

Because we were chattering and laughing so much about this when we reached our clothes on the rocks, a couple behind us, on whom I'd been casting envious eyes because they had a little Primus and a kettle and were brewing tea, suddenly spoke. 'Would you like a cup of tea?' they asked, 'We're just making some and we have plenty.'

'Would we not!' I replied, before Sandy could politely refuse. 'I've been filled with admiration of your stove and kettle since I first caught sight of it.'

They were English, and as we sipped our tea the lady said they'd managed to get an English newspaper. 'Oh, this will be of interest to you,' she said, having indicated she recognized me from TV. 'A friend of yours has just died. But perhaps you knew?'

I took the newspaper from her, and there was a picture of Ruth Drew. 'Suddenly, at a London hospital, Ruth Drew, the well-known specialist in Home affairs and Domestic Economics, after a short illness.'

Like Joan Harben's, Ruth's understated 'not very well' was her final illness.

It had happened three days after we left for Yugoslavia. Deputizing for her was the last thing she was ever to ask of me, and I had refused.

It was a bitter, heart-piercing moment.

It was also the end of *Domestic Forum* for me, for a new producer was brought in, and she decided that all the panel had to be really expert, and to have proper qualifications, with certificates or letters after their names from recognized bodies. So Weir was out on her ear! In her eyes, I was quite definitely one of those whose proper description was 'merely a player'.

Jolly, friendly Rosemary McRobert told me it was all deadly dull without me. All serious replies, and no larks, or fun at all. She couldn't see it lasting. It didn't, well not for very long anyway, so I really didn't miss much.

And as always, when one door shuts, another opens, and I had a lovely series of radio engagements from Scotland in a sort of *Brains Trust*-cum-*Any Questions* which took me to Skye for the first engagement, and this was a real delight, as I'd never visited that romantic island.

The sail from Kyle to Portree was so beautiful that I couldn't bear to miss a minute of it, and kept rushing from one side of the deck to the other, to drink in every little rock and island and cottage to which we seemed to sail so closely that I could almost touch them. The skies were filled with swiftly racing pale grey clouds, and the rocks looked black against them. The captain, seeing my rapt interest, called down to me, 'And are you enjoying yourself, Miss Weir?' 'Oh,' I called back, 'it's so lovely. I can't believe this is my own country, and that I've never seen this part of it before.'

He gazed down at me solemnly, removed his pipe from his mouth and said, 'Do you know, it *is* so bonnie, I find myself admiring it myself, so I do.' I have treasured this remark in my heart. Somehow it says everything about the Scot. Filled with a fierce patriotism, a love of his own land, and yet with a shy apology implied in admitting he finds he looks at its beauty.

The broadcast went well, for how could it do otherwise with such stalwarts as Eric Linklater and George Blake, the novelists, on the platform? All I had to do was supply the feminine point of view. For the law and the scholarly skills Mr Daiches spoke, so I was in very good and brilliant company.

As I had travelled such a distance to fulfil this engagement and it was the lovely month of October I decided that it would only be sensible to take advantage of the fares having been paid, to spend four or five days exploring the island. Sandy was filled with envy that he couldn't accompany me, for he'd never been to Skye either, but he had his office job to do, and we'd already had all the summer holiday to which he was entitled.

Throwing all prudent ideas of economy to the winds, I stayed on in the splendid hotel where the BBC had booked me in for the night of the broadcast, and when the others were on their way back to their various jobs, I was almost alone in my glory in that grand place. It was the first hotel

I'd stayed in where there were combs of honey on the breakfast-table, and where fresh and smoked salmon were regularly on the menu. The waitresses spoke with the soft West Highland accent which is so attractive to the ears, and had delightful old-fashioned ways and tastes. I remember I went to the Gaelic service in the church on the Sunday, for I wanted to savour the strangeness of their customs, and to enjoy the novelty of standing up for the prayers and sitting down for the hymns. There was no music, just a precentor who kept us in tune and started us off at each verse. It was a peculiarly foreign atmosphere to me, for the music of the words simply flowed over me, and were, alas, beyond my understanding.

When I came back to the hotel, the young waitress, a bonnie lass of about eighteen, asked me which church I had gone to. When I told her, she said, 'Och now, I prefer Mr So-and-so myself. You only got a half an hour's sermon with yours, but Mr So-and-so goes on for a full hour.'

I was filled with a sense of wonder that anywhere on this wicked old earth of ours was there to be found a winsome young girl who actually found joy and better value in an hour's sermon, and who of her own free choice preferred this to a mere half-hour somewhere else.

She must have truly gladdened the heart of her minister, and of her God.

The whole populace indeed kept the Sabbath day and considered it an offence if cars were out on the roads. As I had a mere five days to see everything the baker had offered to take me for a run on the Sunday to see a house connected with the famous Flora MacDonald, and I was amazed to see the local people string themselves right across the road so that we had to slow down, and finally stop to let them past. They would not make way for a godless vehicle on the Lord's day. Aye, another world. No wonder they'd been so pleased with me at the broadcast when I'd given it as my opinion that the folk on Skye had every right to refuse tourist crossings on the ferry on a Sunday if they preferred peace and quiet on their own island. The visitors could always come on the Monday, and no harm done.

But their hospitality in every other way was stupendous. When I'd been there only two days, I'd been offered more samples of old John Barleycorn than in the course of several Ne'erdays. When I found myself in a farmhouse at eleven o'clock in the forenoon, it was no surprise to be offered a dram instead of the customary coffee. The farmer's wife looked at me in mild astonishment when I took out my travelling alarm clock and laid it on the arm of the chair.

It was only when she inquired, hesitantly, 'Are you timing your dram, Miss Weir?' that I realized with a shout of laughter that she couldn't know that George the Hostel (so called because he was in charge of the furnace at the children's hostel) had laid magic fingers on my temperamental alarm, and had set it for eleven-thirty a.m. so that it could be tested at once, and that I was merely anxious to have the clock out of my handbag where I could hear it ring. She looked relieved at my explanation and said, 'Och, I thought it wass that you people from the South wass terrible strict with your licensing hours.'

It was she who had recommended the Gaelic service which I'd attended, plus a tinker's funeral on the Monday, which I unfortunately missed, and a dance in the hall that evening which would cost two shillings and would certainly be worth a visit.

After dinner in the hotel a whisky salesman (naturally!) offered to escort me to the dance. His kilt was magnificent, his bonnet set at a rakish angle, and my own dark blue pleated dress seemed very douce and sombre by his side.

Before we left, however, we were hailed by a Glasgow

exile who greeted me as a long-lost friend. He had heard me in the broadcast the night before and, in his opinion, 'I was sticking out a mile'. 'By Goad, he was proud of me,' and he was prepared to fight for the honour of escorting me to the dance.

He had freely imbibed in every hotel in town, by his own confession, and was now in glorious fettle. Without warning, he burst into 'A Gordon for Me' in a fine tenor voice, gazing deeply into my eyes, and I began to doubt the wisdom of attending that dance. However, there was no escape.

He and my kilted salesman stood four-square in the hall until I had collected my coat, and were joined enthusiastically by a venerable old gentleman with white hair who had something to do with the salmon fishing. He was filled with admiration for the way I had daintily sipped my whisky after dinner earlier in the evening, and had said charmingly, 'I'm chust waatching the way you're sipping your whusky, madam – you're chust like a wee burd!'

We all piled into the baker's car and were whirled up the two hundred yards to the hall. It was nearly ten o'clock, but the pictures weren't yet out, and as everybody went to the pictures first and then came on to the dance, the floor was empty.

My Glasgow friend was joined by a bosom pal whom he embraced rapturously. 'Hullo, Willie, by Goad, Willie, come and meet Molly Weir.' Willie was astounded to find me so wee. He had always thought of me as a big fat wifie, he told me, incredulously surveying my tiny physique. 'Well, well, thiss iss a big surprise – and you so wee! It's the voice,' he explained seriously. 'It's the voice. It sounds chust as if it wass coming from a big fat wifie.'

The two accordion players on the platform were joined by a pianist, and they swept gaily into 'My Nut-Brown

Maiden'. I was plunged into the dance by my Glasgow friend, who sang at the top of his voice, nearly drowning the music. He was an unusually fine dancer, and was clearly very much at home on a dance floor.

'Look at us, Willie,' he kept calling out joyously to his pal. 'Look at us.' Willie was obviously used to him, but I was somewhat horrified to find we were still alone on the dance floor, with all the newcomers, as well as Willie and the earlier arrivals, watching our feet with grave attention.

Suddenly he caught sight of a man who had just come in. He stopped as if he'd been shot. 'There's the criminal who dropped the half-bottle on the road last night, Willie,' he called out warningly. 'Don't forgive him, Willie, for ah never wull!'

The dance ended and his brow was damp with sweat, but his eyes were alight with enthusiasm. 'By Goad, Molly, you're a lovely dancer, hen, a lovely dancer.'

'Not as good as my mother, though,' I said modestly. 'She's the dancer in the family.' She was too, and had prizes to prove it.

Another man appeared and my Glasgow friend shook hands with him warmly. They discovered they were fellow Masons. They were quite overcome by this discovery and stood gazing at each other in stupefaction. Willie seized his chance and whisked me into a fierce foxtrot, and we both sang with abandon, 'On the baby's knuckle or the baby's knee, Where will the baby's dimple be?' and he was enchanted to discover he knew all the words.

Pride of Erin followed, then a Gay Gordons, a Boston two-step, a barn dance, with never a pause for breath between. An old man in the corner said with disgust, 'Och, they need a big drum. There is no rhythm without a big drum,' and he started to stamp his feet firmly and noisily in time to the music.

'Shut up,' called out an accordionist fiercely.

'Why should I shut up?' called the old man. 'Shut up yourself. Why should I not beat with my feet when you haf not got a big drum, and nobody can hear the rhythm?' And he stamped on determinedly, sending up little puffs of dust and thoroughly enjoying himself.

I seemed to be the only one there who found this exchange hilarious. Nobody else turned a hair. All points of view, it seemed, were tolerated without rancour, whatever the volume of the shouting.

An old-fashioned waltz found my Glasgow friend as fresh as ever, but my London life was no sort of training for this non-stop marathon and I began to suspect I'd have to be carried home if this furious pace continued.

Seizing a moment when my tireless partner was engaged in remembering yet another pal who was 'one of the finest chaps he ever met', I slipped into the cloakroom and found my coat. The baker, who'd been keeping a watchful eye on proceedings, drove me back to his house, with the kilted whisky salesman, and over a peat fire we had a last dram and a cup of tea before going our various ways.

Before I fell asleep that night I laughed when I compared this Highland reel with the last subdued dance I'd attended in London. What price the quiet Scots, I thought? And how lucky I was to be able to sample an entirely different lifestyle just because of my work.

I visited many other towns with this programme, but nothing ever came up to the sheer entertainment of the Skye visit. I did, though, meet Ishbel MacDonald, the daughter of Ramsay MacDonald, once Prime Minister, when she was in the audience of the broadcast we did from Elgin. She made me laugh when she related how, when she and her father had visited America in connection with the meetings on the naval disarmament proposals, every orchestra played 'Rule Britannia, Britannia Rule the Waves' as they entered, and nobody seemed to see any incongruity in this choice of song. I was very impressed with this tall, quiet, attractive lady, with her nice sense of fun.

On another occasion I travelled on the train with Megan Lloyd George, as I returned to London from a similar broadcast. We recognized one another, she knowing me from TV and me knowing her from her parliamentary appearances. 'By jings,' I thought to myself, with an inner chortle, 'what would my mother and my grannie say to my hobnobbing with the families of men who'd risen to the rank of Prime Minister of Britain?' The amazing thing to me was that they accepted me as one of themselves. But maybe it had something to do with the fact that we were all Celts together?

In the midst of all this travelling, I was still popping back and forth to Glasgow to play the part of Ivy McTweed in *The McFlannels*, and Helen Pryde came up with a bright idea that she and I should capitalize on the fact that we had both lived in Springburn, but with such different backgrounds that we might have inhabited opposite corners of the country. Helen had been brought up in a very God-fearing household, and hadn't even been inside a theatre until she was a married woman. I always had a sneaking suspicion that she was secretly shocked by her own success as a purveyor of Glasgow humour in her marvellous creation, *The McFlannels*.

She once wrote to me, 'Do you ever get frightened by success, Molly? I do. And scared, too, by the haunting fear that I'll soon run out of ideas.'

There must have been a touch of the Jekyll and Hyde about Helen, for while she was writing lines like 'Ye don't appreciate chaps like your Peter – ye stick them on yer chest when you've a cauld' and 'Serah, bring the dug a saucer o' milk' – 'I'll do nothing of the kind – kick it down the stair', she could also write to me in her own neat handwriting, 'My dear Molly, it's the Sabbath day when I don't type.'

I of course had been acting and singing and reciting almost as soon as I could walk and talk, and was taken to the pantomime every Christmas by my enthusiastic mother, who enjoyed the theatre almost as much as I did.

But there were many points at which Helen's experience and mine met, such as Sunday school and bible class, and the discipline of a working-class household. So Helen decided we should do six scripts, of conversation pieces. She wrote her answers to my questions in one script. And I wrote my answers to her questions in the next, and so on. We posted our material back and forward, meeting only on one disastrous occasion in our house in Pinner when poor Walter, Helen's husband, broke every ornament on a wee table which he stepped on while demonstrating some graceful folk-dance they'd seen in Norway! He was shattered, but I've always been pretty handy with the glue-bottle, and there had been worse disasters at sea!

Our next meeting was in Helen's house in Edinburgh, where the BBC recorded the whole six scripts in the course of a single day. Helen played the piano and I sang hymns and the six shows went out on six consecutive Saturdays at a very good listening time.

The critics were very kind to it, although one of them was a bit left-handed in his praise. He said he had listened, prepared to be bored to tears and had thought it started off as a nauseating sample of women chatting together. And then when Helen had said, with the conspiratorial tone of a hardened sinner, 'Molly, did you ever blow up and burst the poke of your Sunday school picnic bag?' he had found himself laughing with the sort of sheer pleasure he'd once known in listening to *Take It From Here*. Praise indeed!

But my mother thought I'd almost got the freedom of the city of Glasgow when I was asked to open the Radio and Television Exhibition, which was held in St Andrew's Hall, now alas burnt to the ground, as I write, but something may yet rise like a phoenix from the ashes.

When I made my opening speech, my picture was transmitted via two hundred screens on sets all over the building. My mink stole came into its own that day, and my mother was thrilled beyond words to have tea with all the VIPs afterwards, to nibble at dainty sandwiches, and have as many French cakes as she fancied. And they presented me with a portable radio set, like a little attaché case, which I have to this day and which still works perfectly. In those days we expected things to last a lifetime, and they usually did.

I think it was the St Andrew's Hall appearance which convinced my mother that I really had something to do with the world of entertainment. It must be serious if the Glasgow folk thought it was worth their while my opening their exhibition. Everybody knew that 'the English', to use my mother's words for Londoners, would believe anything, so nothing surprised her that they did. But the evaluation of her fellow-Glaswegians, well, that was something else again.

This suspicion that there might be something in the idea that I was a real actress, and not just our Molly acting the goat, was confirmed when she saw me for the first time at 'the pictures'. She'd heard me on radio, she'd seen me on TV, but they were in the house after all. She'd only seen me on the stage at the Empire with Henry Hall, and that was again because Henry had seen me in *ITMA*.

But to go to 'the pictures', and see me on the screen,

albeit the part was small, was a revelation to her. She associated the silver screen with Garbo, with Douglas Fairbanks, with Charlie Chaplin and her adored Norma Shearer. A neighbour told me my mother had stared in disbelief the first time she'd seen me walking and talking up there, with a whole cinema looking and listening attentively, not questioning at all my right to be there. My mother had said, 'My Goad, hoo did she ever manage tae get into the pictures? She aye said she wanted to be a film star, and she's managed it.'

To my mother the screen was stardom, however small the part. And the first part was very small. Well, to be honest, I never did play a big part on film, dearly as I loved film acting. But that film she saw was destined to go all round the world, and is still being shown on TV. I get mail from Australia, from Canada, from New Zealand, and friends and relatives tell me of leaping to their feet on catching sight of me and yelling, 'Oh, it's Molly,' much to the amusement of the rest of the audience. It was called *The Silent Witness* and all I and anybody else can remember of it was that it concerned a bicycle! And I earned the magnificent sum of £10 for my work on it.

But from the very first, I loved filming, and I was soon doing what the Americans called 'bit parts' in a score of pictures. Bebe always said I was a natural film actress, with a real feeling for it, for she and I both shared extreme nervousness in all the other acting media, but in films we were just happily nervous and excited: warm and keyed up, truly enjoying the excitement and involvement, with none of the agonies and cold fear which were too often present with other forms of entertaining the public.

For of course it wasn't long before *Life with the Lyons* was the subject of a full-length feature film, but before that there was the glamour of Bebe and Ben's silver wedding.

10

Hollywood marriages were not noted for their durable quality. We knew all about them, for every scrap of film gossip was devoured over here, and we came to believe that it was well-nigh impossible for famous stars to stick to one partner for life. As my dear ma-in-law used to say, reading of yet another divorce, 'They'd put marriage out of the fashion, the way they behave.'

Those who did last the course became legendary, and among the best loved of the couples who seemed to have found the secret of married happiness were our Bebe and Ben.

The public adored them. Not only had they stayed in Britain during the war when they could so easily have returned to the safety of the United States, but they exemplified the old British characteristic of loyalty to one another. So, naturally, when the date of the silver wedding came round there was the widest newspaper coverage since Churchill had lost the election. The entire country seemed interested in devouring every detail, and the press happily supplied stories of their career, of our shows, of what we would wear, of how we got on, etc., etc., and we all seemed to spend hours on the telephone answering reporters' questions.

Bebe and Ben, knowing I was a Scots Presbyterian, threw me into a mutinous tizzy by telling me that the Roman

Catholic Cardinal Griffin would be there to give his blessing, and that I would be required to curtsey to him and kiss the papal ring.

'I'm not going to kiss the ring,' I cried indignantly. 'I'm a Presbyterian.'

'Oh well, then,' said Ben, 'you can just call the whole thing off.' And, turning to May, the secretary, he'd said, 'Cancel that invitation to Molly and Sandy, will you? She's refused to kiss Cardinal Griffin's ring.'

I wasn't sure whether or not he was pulling my leg, for I knew the Catholic Church was full of formalities which had to be observed, and in the end I didn't really know if I would be the only person in the Dorchester who wouldn't kiss that ring until I was actually there, and saw that it wasn't demanded of me at all.

That Ben Lyon! He never could resist teasing me.

They'd booked the Dorchester ballroom, as there would be hundreds of guests, both from all over Britain and from Hollywood. Sandy had a nice new suit, and as far as my dress was concerned, I was in luck. I'd just compèred a fashion show (nothing I did nowadays surprised me!) and they'd designed a lovely pale grey and lemon dress for me, of the newest ruched seersucker-type nylon. I couldn't believe my ears at the end of the show, when I took off the dress and hung it up, to be told that the dress was mine! I'd never expected such generosity. They smiled, 'It's yours,' they said. 'Who else would it fit?'

I was overjoyed. It would be perfect for the Dorchester.

It was a beautiful June day, and the fans lined Park Lane in their hundreds, to watch the famous and the not-so-famous go in.

All the current favourites from the panel games were top of the league as far as the fans were concerned and were met with excited cheering and rapturous approval. Bernard

Braden and Barbara Kelly, whom I was meeting for the first time, as well as Elizabeth Allen, with whom I was later to work on a quiz programme, and of course Isabel, Lady Barnet, who was the queen of *What's My Line?* I found her charming, and great fun, with the unexpected ability to drop into the Glasgow accent when speaking to us, which was quite hilarious matched against her elegant appearance.

We discovered that Wilfred Pickles and Mabel, then at the height of their popularity with their *Have A Go* programme, were shortly to celebrate their own silver wedding, and Ben got a great laugh when he perpetuated the myth of his radio meanness and called them forward after he'd cut the giant wedding cake, and offered to sell them a tier for their own celebrations.

Jack Hulbert and Cicely Courtneidge were there (all Blackpool traumas apparently forgotten!), although I felt a bit of a Judas when I smiled and chatted to Jack, remembering guiltily how I'd prayed that he'd never return to Blackpool to plague and exhaust us. Looking at his easy smiling charm, which contained no hint of reproach at our reactions to him, I marvelled that such a short time ago he seemed to have the power of life and death over us. I don't know whether or not his wife Cicely Courtneidge was aware of the Blackpool backstage dramas, but she was as friendly as could be and showed no inclination to cut me dead!

As Sandy has remarked, of course, actors are like children and can have the most hair-raising scenes which would result in everlasting feuds if one were dealing with 'normal' people. But they can easily forgive and forget, and work just as happily and easily in future productions as though firm friendship had been all that had been experienced between them. Which, when one comes to analyse it, is not surprising for it is precisely their volatile temperament which makes them actors.

It was a great thrill to meet Jack Buchanan and his tall, lovely wife. I made Jack laugh when I told him that the last time I had been in his company was when I came round backstage to the Alhambra theatre in Glasgow when they were auditioning aspirants for small parts for his latest musical comedy, and I'd danced in my walking office shoes and kilt and I'd sung 'The Laird o' Cockpen', when all the other more knowledgeable girls were in leotards, ballet shoes, and had sheet music for their songs. I hadn't known about music and the English pianist hadn't known 'The Laird o' Cockpen' and I'd had to sing unaccompanied in that huge empty theatre.

All Scotland adored Jack Buchanan, who always went back to Arran for his holidays, in spite of having captured the world of light comedy. We thought this showed great loyalty to Scotland, and we gladly queued for seats for his shows, to thrill to his graceful dancing, whimsical comedy, and unmistakable singing style. I was to get to know him much better in the future, but all that lay ahead.

Sandy's greatest moment that afternoon came when he was introduced to Henry Cotton, then the world's best-known golfer. He stared at his hand with a dazed expression when they parted. He was a bit like the girl who refused to wash her face after a famous film star had kissed her! Or like myself when Gene Kelly kissed my cheek! 'To think I've just shaken hands with Henry Cotton,' he said reverently, 'I never thought such a thing could ever happen to me.'

We were both exchanging ooohs and ahhhhs, when Bebe came over and said, 'I want you to meet a great friend of mine, the only one who was at our wedding twenty-five years ago,' and there standing in front of us was Mary Pickford!!!

My mother would never believe it, was my first thought.

Mary of the golden curls, who had been among the first idols of the silver screen.

Mary Pickford, the world's sweetheart.

Somehow, because she was so strongly associated with the legend of the early cinema, when screen goddesses were never imagined to be flesh and blood, her appearance in the Dorchester had the same sort of fantasy as though one of the figures from the paintings on the wall had stepped out of the frame and spoken to us.

I managed to stammer something about it being a great honour to meet the world's sweetheart face to face – and her husband, I added hastily. To which she responded, with an endearing little giggle, that it was a great honour to meet *me* and my husband, honey!

Once married to the great Douglas Fairbanks, she was now the wife of Buddy Rogers, another screen favourite. The Fairbanks–Pickford divorce had shattered the public, for it was a fairy-tale romance smashed to smithereens in the full glare of the press, and people had shaken their heads over her later marriage to the younger Buddy Rogers.

But I didn't care a button just then for divorces, re-marriages, or anything else. I was just fascinated beyond words to be shaking hands with someone who, in my wildest dreams, I never imagined I'd see in the flesh.

She turned to a tall, dark handsome man beside her. 'I'd like you to meet my husband, Buddy Rogers,' she said. She was so tiny, just about my own height in fact, that she could 'coory' against him in playful teasing without even disturbing his breast-pocket handkerchief, which was above the level of her head. She had a light brittle voice, and I dimly remembered that that had been her problem when the talkies came in, for she had been a goddess of the silent screen, and when sound came it was discovered that the public expectations of the voice didn't match up to the image.

She was very American, and talked very fast, and it was difficult at that time for unfamiliar ears to pick up the accent properly.

But she was still very much part of the Hollywood scene, with her shared ownership of film companies and studios, and she was quite adorable, like a perfect little porcelain doll.

It was a really magic moment for us when the legend became flesh.

My mother had to be told every word of this meeting next time I was in Glasgow, and was fascinated to hear that her screen heroine was so small. She was glad Buddy Rogers seemed so nice, and as if he would be good to her, but she still grieved over the divorce. 'Aye, it's a peety a' the same she wisnae still married tae Douglas Fairbanks,' my mother said. 'I'd like tae have heard whit he was like. Ah aye thought he wis great in a' thae adventure pictures, an' they say he did a' his ain stunts.' My mother was well up in screen lore!

This reminded me of a hilarious story Ben had told us about Douglas Fairbanks at the time when they had just finished making the *Robin Hood* film. Fairbanks came to New York for the world première, and the publicity department had thought up a stunt to whet the public appetite for the picture, as well as to demonstrate that the star really performed all the stunts himself and didn't require a 'double' for the dangerous stuff. He was to climb to the top of a thirty-storey building, and stand on the very edge, striking a pose against the sky with stretched bow and lethal arrow.

All the press were there, cameras focused on Fairbanks in his Robin Hood outfit, and as he struck his romantic pose and drew back the arrow in dramatic gesture, the action went further than he'd meant, and the arrow flew towards the heavens, beyond recall. There was a moment's dismay, but in the excitement of making sure all the cameras had got what they wanted, they thought nothing more of it. What harm could it do, after all, at that height?

Next day all the papers carried excellent pictures of the intrepid hero atop the skyscraper.

Three days later Fairbanks had a writ served on him. From an injured tailor!

It appeared that this little tailor had been sitting sewing on top of his work-table, with the window open because it was a very hot day, in his workroom at the top of a skyscraper. The next moment, like a missile from the celestial spheres, an arrow had plunged into his bottom!

Five thousand dollars were paid out of court.

Ben used to curl up with laughter when he came to this part. 'Can you imagine it, honey?' he'd splutter to me. 'This little guy sitting there sewing, thirty storeys up, when an arrow flies through the open window, straight into his bottom. I can just see him,' Ben would go on, 'looking up as if it were a bolt from heaven and saying, "How in hell did that get here? Where'd it come from?" and then the next day opening his newspaper and realizing at once he'd been shot by Robin Hood.' Ben would laugh again. 'He sure knew where to sue the minute he saw those pictures.'

My mother enjoyed that tale, and she was certain the wee tailor, once he'd got over the shock, had earned that five thousand dollars a lot easier than sitting making suits for a living. 'Mind you,' she said in some wonder, 'I'd never have thought masel' o' such a thing, but maybe somebody tellt him about suing. As sure as daith, ye can make money oot o' onything nooadays. Och, but the wee soul deserved it for the fright he must have got.'

But although Douglas Fairbanks hadn't been at the silver wedding, somebody else was there whom I found it just as exciting to meet, and that was the current heart-throb Tyrone Power. Barbara introduced me. There were so many famous, identifiable faces in that room, that even a face like Tyrone Power's could remain unnoticed until one focused one's attention as directed. 'Oh, there's Ty Power,' said Barbara. I jumped with excitement, hardly believing I hadn't seen and picked him out among the half-dozen people at the bar. I was struck by Barbara's use of the shortened version of his name, a sure sign they were on personal friendly terms, and in a moment I was shaking hands, and looking into the romantic brown eyes which had previously only gazed into mine from the movie screen. He had been filming abroad and was deeply tanned, with perfect white teeth, and intensely black hair. He was very quiet in his manner, and every bit as gorgeous as he appeared on the screen. He was probably dead tired after months of filming, but I always equated quietness with gentility and I was very impressed. He and Barbara exchanged 'Hi's' and 'How're things?' while I just stood and drooled. It was enough for me just to look.

I was dizzy with rubbing shoulders with the great, and the surest proof of my euphoria is that I can't remember a single thing that I ate that afternoon.

I only know that Sandy and I sat staring into space all the way back to Pinner, filled with our individual memories of that unforgettable silver wedding. I don't think I could have eaten much at the Dorchester, for I suddenly found that I was starving.

I wondered if the little gift we had made from the cast to commemorate this special day had pleased them, for it was a very small token measured against the delights offered to us by them. But what do you give to people like Bebe and Ben, who not only have everything, but who also have the means of buying whatever takes their fancy?

We had talked it over amongst ourselves, Horace Percival, Doris Rogers, Hugh Morton and I, and had decided to give a combined memento, which would be a reminder that we in the cast had shared their happy day. I volunteered to choose something from a special little antique shop in Pinner, which I could return if they didn't approve.

With the help of the owner I selected a silver sweet dish shaped like the ace of clubs, with a very attractive moulding in the design, and Bebe and Ben were absolutely delighted. We know they liked it, for it was in use in their drawing room all the time thereafter and we saw it every time we went to their house in Southwick Street.

I solved the problem of presents at Christmas and on birthdays by deciding on something I knew they'd never have the time to do for themselves, and which had the added pleasure of having been the result of my own handi-work. I grew bulbs for them. Bebe adored growing flowers, although she always forgot when she ought to have seen to their planting, and she was always as enchanted with my bowl of about-to-bloom hyacinths as though I'd given her a diamond necklace. With their central heating the flowers were out weeks ahead of mine, and I was invited along to see their progress and to sniff at their fragrance, which truly filled the room.

Once when she was ill, I gave them an amaryllis by way of a change, and Ben told me they'd had the greatest fun watching it shoot up like a poker towards the ceiling, growing about an inch in a day it seemed. And in the end when it burst forth into a magnificent flame-colour lily they were absolutely stunned by its beauty, and by the sheer surprise of the almost artificial perfection of the petals.

I hit upon Bebe's favourite flower quite by accident. In our garden at that time we had a clump of lily of the valley which had crept through from the garden next door, and rioted all over the bed near the fence. It always came weeks before anyone else's, even before the neighbour's from whose original planting it had come, and one day on impulse I picked a large bunch on my way to the Paris where we were doing our recording, and I handed them to Bebe as a little gift from our garden. She buried her face in them, and closed her eyes in rapture. 'Oh, Aggie, how did you know? They are my favourite flower!'

Ben was staring at them in amazement. 'Where'd you get them from, Aggie?' he asked. 'And how did you know it was Mommy's birthday?' I hadn't known, but I knew now. What a piece of luck.

They'd scarcely believe they were from our garden, until Ben as usual turned the tables and teased me by saying, 'They must be from her garden. They're fifteen shillings for half a dozen stems from Moyses Stevens today, and old Scotch wouldn't pay that! A bunch that size would cost pounds.'

Flowers were the only things which aroused Bebe to true joy, in the way of a present, for she had little time for material things, and was happiest working away on the script.

From then on, she had a bunch of our lily of the valley every year for her birthday. Later, when Barbara had a garden of her own and was deep in garden-lore culled from books, she began to tell me one day at rehearsal that my lilies of the valley were growing in quite the wrong conditions.

Ben turned at once. 'You leave Aggie alone,' he said. 'She knows what she's doing. If she can bring your mother a vaseful for her birthday every year, when the shops are asking a fortune for a few stems, she's right and the books are wrong!'

It was the most enjoyable feeling being able to be sure that I could provide something money couldn't easily buy, from our own wee garden, with the full scent and beauty of an unforced flower.

Bebe and Ben always reflected real life in their stories, so we were soon involved in a fine old romp celebrating the silver wedding, in the film *The Lyons in Paris*.

We'd already done *Life with the Lyons* on film, which was extremely successful, and for me it was the greatest experience working with stars of their quality. I was fascinated to discover the extent of their knowledge. The technicalities were child's play to them. Not just the lighting, and which was their 'best' side from the camera's point of view, but where to make an effective cut, and why they couldn't walk out of that scene because it wouldn't match the next one.

I was quite staggered, for I know nothing of that side of the business, and just go on and do my scene, implicitly trusting that camera, sound, direction, lighting and everything else will fall into the right places to make the perfect 'take'.

Bebe had been in films from the age of thirteen, when it was expected that actors did their own stunts and worked right round the clock, and what she hadn't learned then wasn't worth knowing. She'd been a world star at seventeen, and had absorbed more knowledge of the industry than almost anyone else with whom she was now working.

Ben, after giving up Hollywood films as an actor, had been appointed casting director for 20th Century Fox, and as almost everyone now knows had been the one to discover Marilyn Monroe and put her under contract for the studio. He continued as casting director for 20th Century Fox in London for many years, and had been in on the big decisions with the top brass for years.

Ben could 'time' the number of frames to a scene, and was instantly aware of what would and what would not cut well.

They amazed me, both of them.

Richard had done quite a lot of filming in Hollywood as a youngster, and had been in *Anna and the King of Siam* with Rex Harrison, a part he had thoroughly enjoyed and remembered with pleasure. He was now grown up, or so he thought, in his late teens and was in the throes of a romantic attachment with Jill Ireland, a starlet who came to the shows a great deal, and who occasionally featured in the radio series as Richard's girl friend.

But she didn't appear in the film. Belinda Lee was chosen to play the ingénue who has a crush on Richard and whom he flees from, because she depicted the hearty, horsy, toothy type. In real life, she'd just become engaged to Cornel Lucas, a very well-known photographer, and was a lovely English blonde with great screen appeal. I profoundly admired her rose-leaf complexion, perfect teeth (I always noticed teeth, coming from 'toothless' Glasgow!) and thick strong hair, and we struck up a happy friendly relationship.

I remember one night she had an appointment to see a famous director at the Dorchester, and was going on straight after our day's filming. She was in a great tizzy about this, and had rushed along to Bourne and Hollingworth on her few hours off and had bought a black taffeta cocktail dress specially for that evening. This was entirely against my mother's edict that you never bought anything in a hurry, or wore it at once to meet anybody, for you always looked more 'yourself' in something which was comfortable and which had worked itself into your movements, so it was your personality which came over and not the dress's.

Belinda, listening to all this from me as I helped her into her nine-guinea taffeta, was unrepentant. 'But I don't want to look "myself",' she said. 'I want to look like a glamorous film star. Now should I put my hair up, or keep it down?'

She wound her hair up, looked at herself from every

angle. Took it down again and brushed it out. Put it up again, this time in a more casual swirl. I was with her every step of the way, for I knew how vital it was to make a good impression. They would judge her on her first appearance as she walked through the door.

Finally we both decided hair up was more chic, threw our arms round one another in 'Good luck, and good night', Belinda speeding towards the Dorchester, me towards Pinner and Sandy who, needless to say, was regaled with the whole story and who decided she must be strong as a horse to undertake such a journey and such a meeting after a day's filming.

The following day I learned that the director had liked her, and had promised there might be a part for her in his next picture, which would be made in Italy. 'Oh, Belinda,' I breathed enviously, 'how lucky. I've only ever been on location in Regent's Park, and you'll go all the way to Italy, with your fare paid. You can have a wee holiday afterwards, to make the most of such a gorgeous job, if it comes off.'

The next news I had, long after our film was finished, was that Belinda's engagement had been broken off, and she was on her way to Italy to make a film. So she had got the part after all! I wondered if the film had been the cause of the ending of the romance with Cornel. Well, that was one engagement which hadn't lasted long. I was amazed at how light-heartedly such things could be ended, after all the fuss the newspapers had made of them. I'd have been affronted at appearing so fickle, so soon, but then I was used to the long, unbreakable engagements of my Scots friends, and I didn't realize that newspaper gossip of show business romances was forgotten almost as soon as the paper had been used for lighting the fire.

But from time to time I would see pictures of Belinda in

the newspapers, looking more and more voluptuous, in scanty bikinis, and in provocative poses. When I remembered her modestly turning her back to me to slip into her simple little black taffeta, it didn't seem possible that I was looking at the same girl. She was still very beautiful, but had I ever given this torrid-looking female advice about her hair? Or zipped her into a Bourne and Hollingworth dress costing under £10? Had we really queued together for a cup of tea and a roll sandwich from the caravan on the film set? She looked so expensive and exotic now, that she might have been a creature from another planet, not one into whose dressing room I could casually pop to have a chat and a laugh.

Then scandal broke, in the highest places.

An Italian prince, one of the papal Counts to the Vatican, had been forbidden to continue his duties unless his relationship with Belinda Lee was terminated. Not only was he a papal Count, he was a husband and father, and it was a disgrace on all scores.

I simply couldn't associate the Belinda I knew with all this *dolce vita*. Italy had surely unbalanced her, just as her blonde beauty had taken Italy and an Italian prince by storm.

The last item the newspapers carried was on the front page. My heart turned over when I saw her picture there. Underneath it said, 'Killed in a car crash, British actress Belinda Lee, whose affair with an Italian prince has been one of the most talked-about scandals in recent years.'

It was the classic, terrible end to high living, rich men and fast cars.

She had whizzed into prominence with the dazzling brilliance of a Roman candle, and had just as quickly been burnt out and fallen to earth.

It was a tragic waste.

Our films were such a success that it seemed inevitable that we would be asked to transfer our radio comedy show to TV, for television was going from strength to strength, and already people were tending to find their entertainment within their own four walls. It was obvious there was a tremendous TV future for comedy shows starring well-tried favourites from radio, but at first the BBC cautiously booked us for a modest four half-hour shows.

For each production we had ten days' rehearsal, and two days in the studio, and with Bebe and Ben's film expertise, each show was handled as though it were a film, with the added bonus that we had ten days to get everything right.

Against a lot of the trial and error experimenting that was going on in TV at that time, the Lyons' half-hour shows had the gloss of a Hollywood product. Nothing was skimped. Perfection was demanded, and, as far as was humanly possible, obtained. The shows were an instant success. The newspapers were unanimous in their welcome. 'Fast, slick and funny.' 'How successfully the Lyons' show has transferred from radio to TV. All the gang are there, in great form.'

And when the third one of the four had been seen, there was an article in heavy type which asked, 'What is Lime Grove going to do about the Lyons' series which is due to end on August 10th? It mustn't be allowed to finish. The Lyons, with Molly Weir and Horace Percival, have brought the sort of comedy into our homes that viewers have been needing for years.'

By Jove, these were pleasant words to read, for Bebe and Ben always strove for good clean family fun, and although we had worked hard, it was a fact that not all radio shows transferred happily to vision. It seemed that ours had. It also seemed that we would very definitely have to divide our year between TV and radio, to keep a toe in both camps as it were. For the Lyons still greatly valued their radio success, and they loved to feel they were providing a jolly, wholesome show which could be heard by all the family without a blush or an explanation.

Meantime there was a brief hiatus between this short TV series ending and the next radio series starting at the end of September, and I was offered a very nice part in a film to be made in full colour called *John and Julie*.

This was the story of two children who had run away to see the Coronation, and I had a private suspicion, although I was delighted to be in the film, that it was rather a long time after the event for it to make much of a hit. How wrong I was. It was a sensational success in America, it took an Oscar for its writer-director, and had rave notices wherever it was shown. Looking at the cast list now, one can see how many first-rate actors were involved in it, although in the scenes which included me I only met one or two of them. Moira Lister, Wilfrid Hyde White, Sid James, Megs Jenkins, Constance Cummings, Andrew Cruickshank, Winifred Shotter (of the Aldwych farces), Peter Jones, Peter Sellers, Mona Washbourne, Russell Waters, Bill Shine – to name but a few! And the commentary was by Richard Dimbleby and Wynford Vaughan Thomas.

At that time the British film industry was booming, and I seemed to be haring all over the place, to studios within a twenty-mile radius. None of the parts was very big, but I was gaining valuable experience working for many directors, and I loved everything about the film industry. Except the crack-of-dawn rising! I never got used to that, and was thankful I was not the type who would ever be asked to play love scenes, for I could never have summoned up enough enthusiasm to do them justice at nine o'clock in the morning!

I did have an enjoyable part as a servant where I had to be alarmed out of bed by a supposed burglar, and I used to undress the minute I reached the studios, get into nightie and dressing gown, have my make-up put on, and then sit up in bed having a second breakfast, handed to me by one of the carpenters. It was even possible to enjoy a bit of a snooze while the scene was being lit. That was great fun, and I was being paid for it into the bargain!

At Teddington I worked with Joan Greenwood and André Morell, who met and fell in love while we were making this film, and were later married. I found it very exciting to be in at the beginning of this romance, and I found Joan's fragile beauty very striking. Although I've always been considered very small and slim, beside Joan I felt a great hulking brute. Small-boned, with a long delicate neck, tiny wrists and fine silky hair, she looked as if a puff of wind would blow her away. She had a delicious sense of humour, and she kept me in constant giggles during our canteen lunches. She was very struck by my amiable acceptance of the fact that everyone greeted me by imitating my Scottish accent, and was appalled to remember she had done the self-same thing when she'd been introduced to me.

'I'll never do such a thing again,' she promised, 'for I can see how *infuriating* it must be. I must say you take it much better than I would.' All this was delivered in her husky, elegant tones, which made everything she said sound witty and significant in my ears.

Over at Walton I worked for Denis O'Keefe from Hollywood in *Million Dollar Diamond*, and again at Walton I worked for the great Ken Annakin in *Value for Money* which starred John Gregson, Diana Dors and Donald Pleasance. This was a very enjoyable picture, and it was especially nice to have been asked to work again for Mr Annakin, who'd made a little documentary starring yours truly when I'd first come to London. That had been an educational film, not for public cinema showing, but even then he was clearly a talent to be reckoned with, and he later went on to do great work in British films.

It was during the making of that film that I was introduced to Richard Burton's first wife, Sybil, and it's amazing what a difference it makes when you've actually met someone, when you later hear that she's been left in favour of another woman. I only met Sybil that once, but she was a real person to me after that lunch we all shared, and I couldn't be indifferent to her fate when Burton fell in love with Elizabeth Taylor. Sybil later made her own future, but for a while I suffered with her all the blinding publicity of that affair, just because our lives had briefly touched.

I had come to the capital chiefly to see what I could do in the world of films and television, and in the West End theatre. The theatre seemed to be taking a back seat, but I was getting so much work in the other media that I now had to keep a cuttings book, and two engagement diaries, one for professional bookings and one for private engagements.

When one is so busy as this, it seems impossible that it will ever come to an end. But of course it has to end some day. But not for a long, long time, please God, I thought.

I had enlarged my horizons considerably since I had stepped tentatively into the Lyons' Den. And there were years and years stretching ahead. I hoped. But could one ever be sure?

The last seven years had certainly been action-packed. But I wasn't counting any chickens. I knew only too well how the bubble of popularity could burst without warning.

Another Hogmanay was coming up. What lay ahead? I longed to be able to pierce the veil which shrouded the future.

Then my mother asked me, in her Christmas letter, 'What was yon lovely verse the King once spoke, in his Christmas message just when the war started?'

And I wrote back to her the words which had made such a profound impression on the listening nation:

And I said to the man who stood at the gate of the year, 'Give me a light that I may tread safely into the unknown,' and he replied, 'Go out into the darkness and put your hand into the hand of God. That shall be to you better than light and safer than a known way.'

What had made my mother ask me for those words at this particular time?

Whatever the reason, by reminding me of them she had all unwittingly stilled my curiosity about the untrodden paths which lay ahead. Wherever they led, uphill or down dale, I determined to tackle whatever I met in the way of good fortune or bad with courage and cheerfulness, and faith.

I'd put a guid stout heart to the steepest brae.

One step at a time.

That was the thing.

If you would like a complete list of Arrow books please send a postcard to P.O. Box 29, Douglas, Isle of Man, Great Britain.